by Alan Brown

LEARNING-DOING SAILING MANUAL
INVITATION TO SAILING
INVITATION TO SAILBOAT RACING

INVITATION TO SAILBOAT RACING

A Programmed Series of Lessons in Sailing Tactics and Racing Strategy

ALAN BROWN

Simon and Schuster
New York

Published by Simon and Schuster
Rockefeller Center, 630 Fifth Avenue
New York, New York 10020

First printing

sbn *671-20987-6*
Library of Congress Catalog Card Number: 70-154095
Designed by Jack Jaget
Manufactured in the United States of America

Contents

In Memoriam

There were many facets to the brilliance of Alan Brown. As a student at Cornell University, he showed glints of promise as a painter, sculptor, news editor, leader of men. In his first job, in advertising, he shone with promise; but he chose to rephase his goals and achieve a career as a physician.

In the few years he practiced medicine, his warm understanding, his creative leadership, his abilities as a teacher did much to endear him to the people he served.

Throughout his varied and interesting life, Alan Brown was always, from early childhood, a sailor. Boats and water to sail them on were a thread of continuity, were the fiber of his person. He learned carpentry so that he could build a boat. Wartime service to his country meant enlistment in the Coast Guard, in which he was accepted into the Academy. He once had the fortune to crew on the *Eagle* in the Bermuda Race.

His poetry was the sun and clouds and the breeze that filled the sail. To him the perfect sculpture was a beautiful hull, and his favorite picture was a photograph of his Herreshoff 28 at rest in an autumn-colored bay. His respect for his fellowman showed in the race won honestly, or lost with good grace. His appreciation of excellence led him to hard work done to earn the very best Comet built, and he showed love in the way he cared for her.

His first teaching was to a class of junior sailors he formed to provide permanence for a declining yacht club. The project a success, he went on to enlarge and market the sailing manual he had written, and to teach similar courses at other yacht clubs.

His *Invitation to Sailing* was written at night, after his duties as a medical resident were finished for the day. At the same time, he laid out the theme of *Invitation to Sailboat Racing*; but it was not until six years later, after he was stricken with his fatal illness, that he put it into a final format. Weakened but undaunted, he dictated this book to a number of friends and to members of his family, who in serving him found that their own lives became somehow richer.

He died May 26, 1970, leaving an almost completed manuscript.

Introduction /

One of the greatest pleasures for the experienced sailor, and one of the greatest mysteries for the beginner, is sailboat racing.

It is here in the small boats on lakes and bays that the thrills of competition are so rewarding. Here the young skipper makes the wind and water work to his advantage — and measures it against the advantage of his best friend.

Racing is not so complicated as to be a mystery for long — yet it is never completely fathomed, and the good sailor is a student of racing as long as he sails.

The purpose of this book is to simplify the mystery of sailboat racing for the beginner, and to refresh the principles of strategy and tactics for the expert.

How to Use This Book

The lessons given in *Invitation to Sailboat Racing* are designed to take the novice sailor from the fundamentals of racing tactics to the point where he is thinking three or four maneuvers ahead.

Each lesson and figure is numbered. When a question is asked, the number has a *Q* after it; and when an answer is given, the number is followed by an *A*. If no letter is present, the material is simply explanatory.

The answers are shown immediately after each problem, on the same or the following page. For this reason it is best to read with the lower portion of the page covered with a card, until an answer is chosen.

The problems are programmed in a definite order for greatest learning and comprehension; the beginning sailor is therefore advised to be thoroughly familiar with Parts I and II before going on. The intermediate sailor may begin with Part II, and the advanced racing skipper may open the book and test his knowledge anywhere.

The racing rules, as set forth by the North American Yacht Racing Union, are presented in part in the Appendix. These will be referred to by number. The reader is encouraged to study them on his own. Not all of the 70-plus racing rules and definitions are discussed in this text, since many deal with protocol, professional crews, or other matters that need not concern the small-boat racer.

PART I

*The Race Course
Completing the Course
Rules Which Apply
Start and Finish Lines*

In this section are shown the various courses that are commonly used in small-boat racing. Explanations and questions are given for the rules that govern the course and rounding marks.

If you're not sure how to tell on which side of a mark to go, what to do if you go around the wrong way, or what to do if you hit the committee boat, then read on.

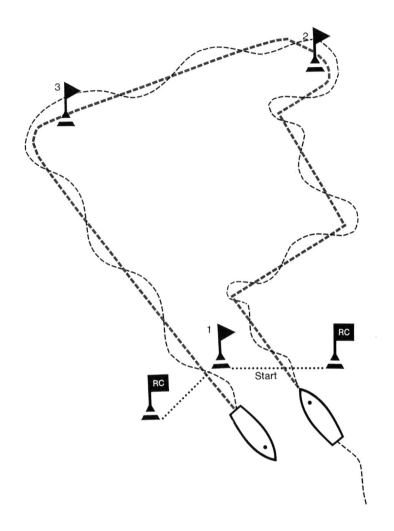

1. To begin with, boats race around a course which consists of
   two or more flags or marks.
   In addition, a boat must round all marks in such a way
   that an imaginary string in its wake, if pulled tight, would
   bring all the marks together.

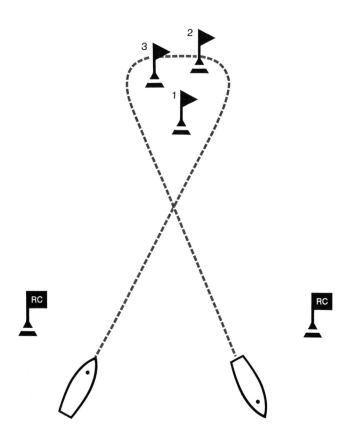

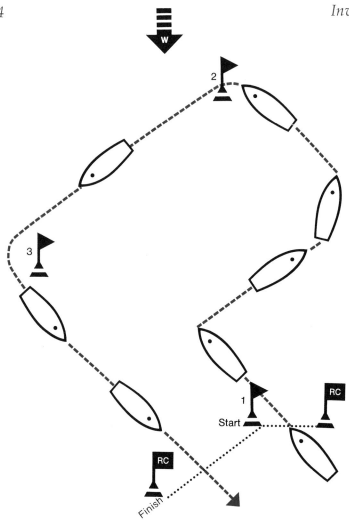

2. The basic race course is a triangle of three flags or marks. The *start* and *finish* are at the same mark. Notice that the Race Committee boat shifts position for the finish line.

Whenever possible, the finish line is adjusted to be at right angles to the last leg of the course, and to allow boats to pass the finish mark on the same side as other marks.

If the local Race Committee decides against this and announces it prior to the *start*, the starting and finish lines may be the same.

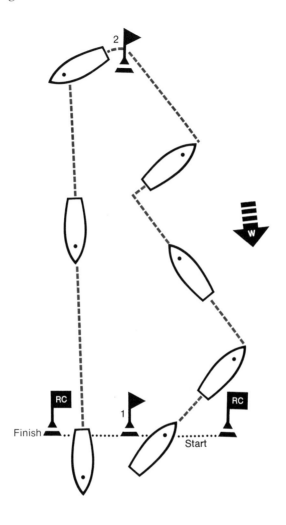

3. An alternative racing course has two marks — one up to windward and one to leeward. This is known as a windward-leeward course.

In both courses the first leg is set into the wind, and is called the windward leg or weather leg. The portion downwind is called the leeward leg.

16

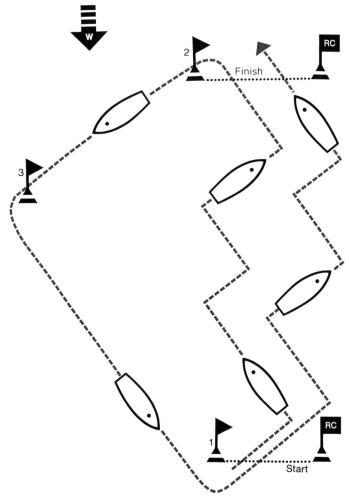

4-Q. Here some elements of both triangular course and windward-leeward course are combined. Which of the following are true?

☐ There is a complete triangle.
☐ There is a complete windward-leeward course.
☐ All marks of the course are passed on the same side.

4-A. This popular course finishes to windward on a beat. The downwind leg of the windward-leeward course is absent, but there is a complete triangle and all marks are passed on the same side.

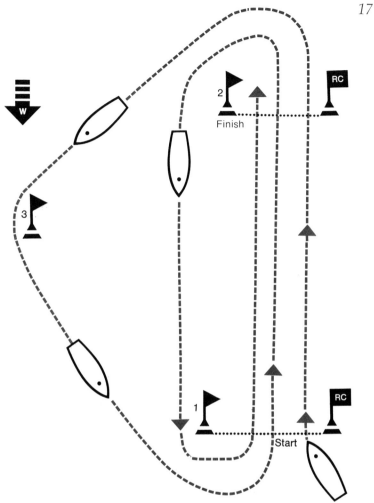

5. This is called an Olympic course. This is the most competitive course, because it provides three windward legs with a
combination of reach and run. Again, finish line is to windward, which adds the third beat, and permits easier reading
of sail numbers by the Race Committee.

All marks are passed on the same side throughout the
course. Here they are left to port.

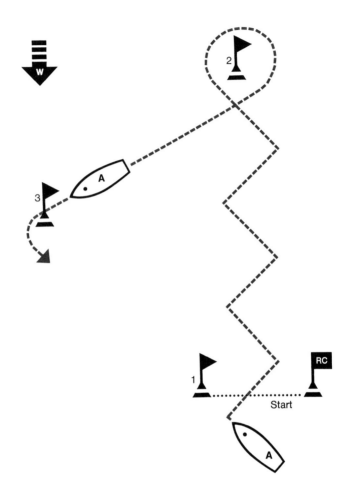

5-Q. Boat A has passed mark No. 2 to starboard instead of to port.

  ☐ Boat A is disqualified.
  ☐ Boat A is disqualified, but may go back to mark No. 2 and correct her error. If true, show how.

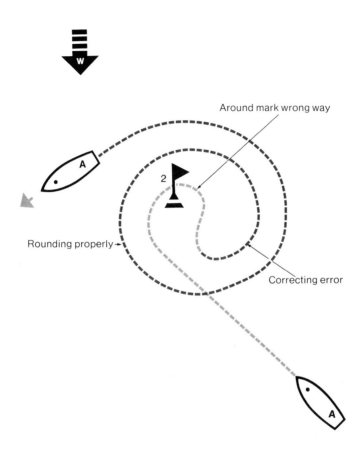

Around mark wrong way

Rounding properly →

Correcting error

5-A. Boat A may return to the mark and correct her error, but must then round properly. If she continues in the race without doing this, she is disqualified.

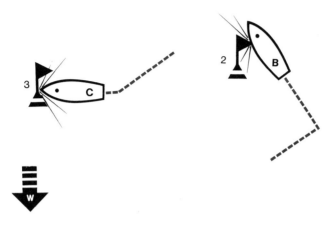

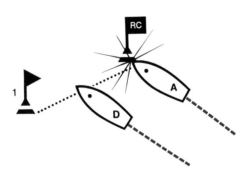

6-Q. After the start, Boat A strikes the Race Committee boat. Boats B and C hit marks.

☐ Boats B and C are disqualified, but A is not, since she only hit the Race Committee boat.

☐ All three boats are disqualified.

☐ All three are disqualified, but may make correcting maneuvers and remain in the race.

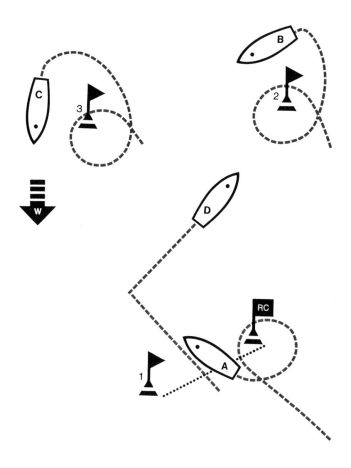

6-A. All three boats are disqualified until they make one penalty turn around the mark and then pass correctly (NAYRU
Rule 52.1). While making this turn, a boat has no rights and
must keep clear of others at the mark (NAYRU Rule 45.1).
At the start or finish line, the penalty turn is made out-
ward from the course.

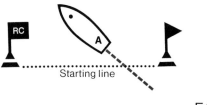

Starting line

WEST   EAST

7-Q. Sometimes the most obvious details escape us. All Boat A found out about this race was that it is a triangle course. How will she pass each mark?

☐ Leave them to port.
☐ Leave them to starboard.

Which mark is the next one she will pass?

☐ The northwest mark.
☐ The northeast mark.

To which side of the starting line will the finish line be shifted?

☐ West of it.
☐ East of it.

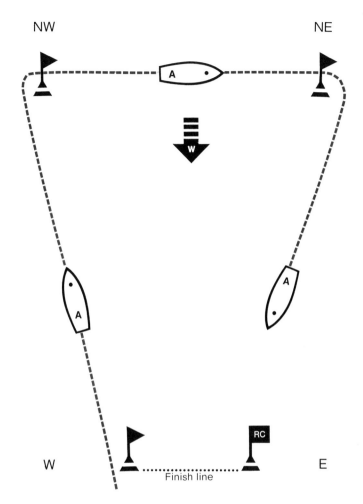

NW   NE

W   E

Finish line

7-A. Since Boat A passed the first mark of the course, the free flag on the opposite end of the line from the Race Committee, on her starboard side, she will pass all marks the same way.

To have a clear triangle, the next mark will be the northwest one. The finish line will be moved east, and boats will sail around the course in a clockwise fashion.

All this information is gained from how the starting mark is passed!

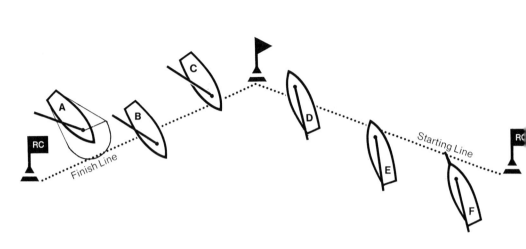

8-Q. When does a boat start or finish a race?

Boat A's spinnaker is over the line, but no part of her hull has crossed. Boat B's mast has crossed; Boat C's mast has not.

☐ Only Boat B has finished.
☐ Both Boats B and C have finished.
☐ All three have finished.
☐ None has finished.

At the starting line, Boat D's mast is over the line; Boat E's mast is not. Boat F's bowsprit is over, but no other part of her hull is over the line.

Who has started?

☐ Only Boat D.
☐ Boats D and E.
☐ All three boats.
☐ None.

8-A. All three boats have finished and all three boats have started. Each has some part of her hull, crew, sails, or equipment over the finish line or starting line, and this is all that is required for an official start or finish.

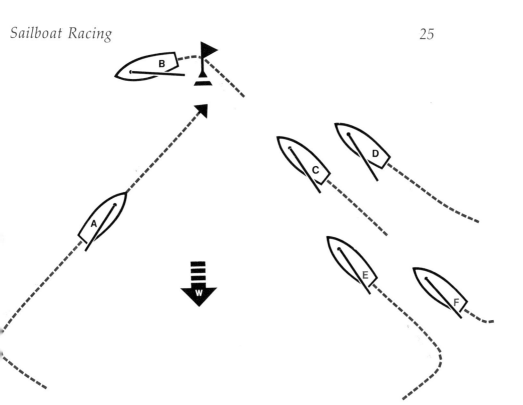

9-Q. The "lay line" is an imaginary line which shows the course a close-hauled boat would sail to fetch a mark. The lay line for port tack is at right angles to the lay line for starboard tack. The two lines meet on the same side of the mark on which the boats will pass.

    1. Which boat has overstood the lay line?
    2. Which boats are on the lay lines?
    3. Which boat has tacked short of the lay line?
    4. Which boats will be able to fetch the mark?

9-A. 1. Boat D has overstood the lay line.
    2. Boats A, C and F are on the lay lines.
    3. Boat E has tacked short of the lay line.
    4. Boats A, C, D and F will be able to fetch the mark. Boat B has already fetched it. Boat E may have to tack once more.

PART II

*The Six Basic Rules and
How to Use Them
Cutting a Competitor's Wind
Blanket Zone and Backwind
Maneuvering at the Marks*

In order to race, a skipper must know the rules. These are set by the North American Yacht Racing Union and are found in part in the Appendix.

Over the years a racing skipper will become familiar with them if he sails well and is involved in one or more protest meetings. A constant review of the racing rules is advisable, as they are revised every four years.

There are over 70 racing rules and definitions, but the most important ones can be lumped under six titles:

1. The Opposite Tack Rule (NAYRU Rule 36)
2. The "Tacking Too Close" Rule (NAYRU Rule 41)
3. The Same Tack Rule (NAYRU Rule 37)
4. The "Buoy Room" Rule (NAYRU Rule 42.1)
5. The "Anti-Barging" Rule (NAYRU Rule 42.1[e])
6. The "Over Starting Line Early" Rule (NAYRU Rule 44)

Knowledge of these six rules will let you begin racing, since they cover 90 percent of all the problems you will encounter. They can be used to your advantage if you know how, and showing you how is the objective of Part II.

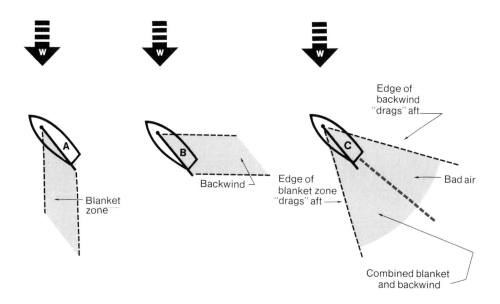

10. When a boat is beating, the wind on her sails produces an area of dead air to leeward, called the blanket zone (Boat A). It also produces a backwind of air which bounces off the sail to windward (Boat B).

    When the boat is under way, these two areas combine to form a single cone of disturbed air which trails behind.

    On a beat, this cone of bad air consists mostly of strong backwind. It is a very effective weapon with which to slow other boats.

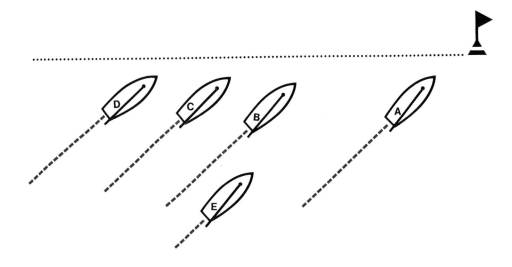

10-Q. Boats A, B, C, and D are even at the start. Within a few boat lengths their positions will shift because of the backwind or blanketing effect.

☐   Boat A will be ahead of all others.
☐   Boats A and B will be ahead of all others.
☐   Boats B, C, and D will remain even with one another, but will be ahead of both A and E.

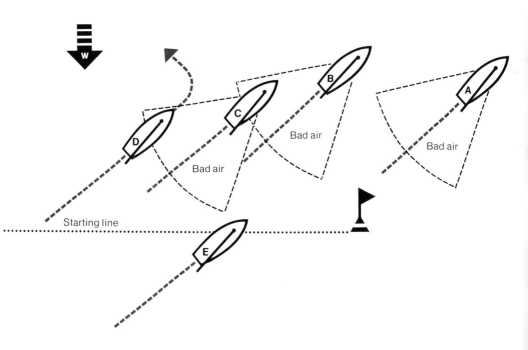

10-A. Boats A and B pull ahead. The backwind from Boat B slows C, and the backwind from Boat C slows D.

Boats A and B have their wind clear and move ahead. Boat E is blanketed by Boats A, B, and C. Boat D is the only one in a position to tack and clear her wind.

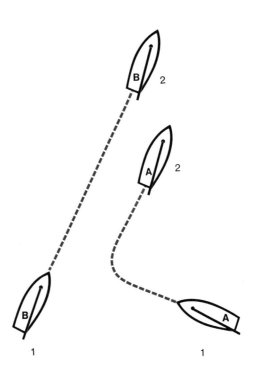

11-Q. Boat B was about to cross the bow of Boat A when Boat A tacked on her leeward side. What should Boat B do now?

☐ Boat B should tack at once.
☐ Boat B should do nothing; A is the one in trouble.
☐ Neither boat is in trouble.

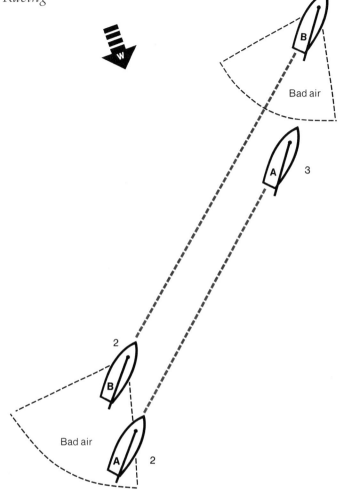

11-A. Boat B should do nothing, since A is in trouble. Boat A has tacked directly into Boat B's cone of disturbed air.

This combination of blanketing and backwind from Boat B ahead destroys the effective driving force of the wind on A's sails, and she slips behind.

In fact, if Boat A tacks again to get clear air, Boat B should tack also to cover her and give her bad air on the other tack.

This offensive tactic is a good means of keeping a close competitor from getting ahead of you.

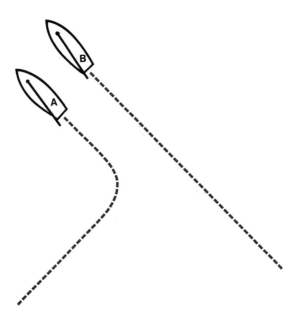

12-Q. Boat A has come about to let the starboard-tack boat (B)
go by. Both boats have the same sailing speed.

☐ · Boat A will backwind Boat B.
☐ Boat B will blanket Boat A.
☐ Boat A has tacked into a safe position.

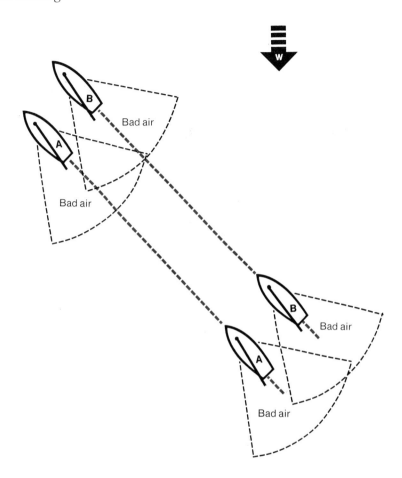

12-A. Boat A has tacked into a Safe Leeward Position (SLP). The cone of bad air from either boat does not affect the other (notice that Boat A is farther ahead with respect to Boat B than was the situation in Fig. 11-Q).

   The Safe Leeward Position is often used by boats in close quarters, especially at the start. Each boat must be careful, however, not to be caught by the other's bad air.

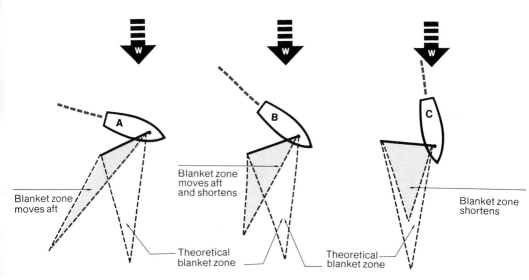

13. On a broad reach or a run, a boat's most effective weapon is blanketing. Backwind plays no part except on the closer reaches.

On a beam reach, Boat A's blanket zone trails well aft. As she moves to a broad reach (Boat B) or a run (Boat C), this blanket zone moves farther forward, but shortens.

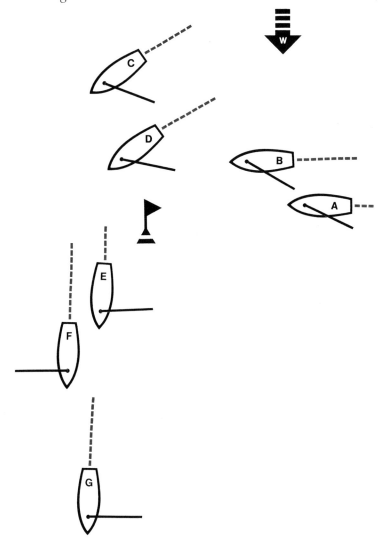

13-Q. In this race, the boats are turning the reaching mark. Which boats are blanketed?

☐ Only Boat A is blanketed.
☐ Only Boat G is blanketed.
☐ Boats A, D, F, and G are blanketed.

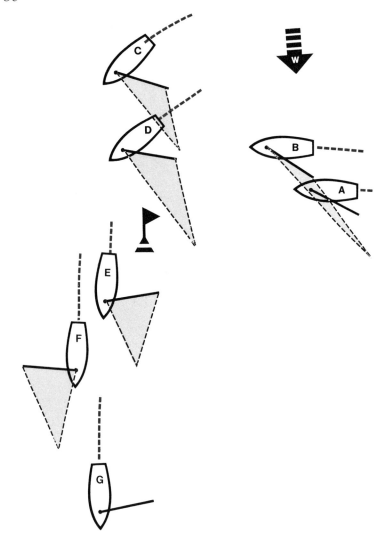

13-A. Only Boat A is blanketed for certain. (She also receives some backwind.)

    The forward speed of Boat C causes her blanket zone to move aft and miss Boat D. On the run, the shortened blanket zones of Boats E and F will not affect Boat G.

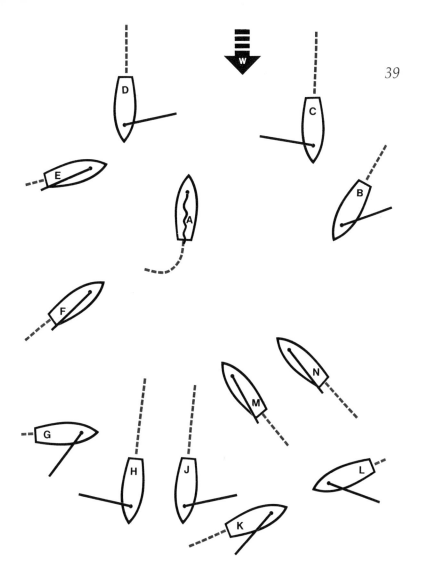

14-Q. It is often necessary to know quickly which tack a nearby boat is on.

It may seem elementary, but one can remember that the tack is named for the side opposite the boom. This is the side the wind comes over to reach the sail (the windward side).

Try these. On which tack are Boats A through N?

14-A. Boats B, D, J, L, M, and N are on starboard tack.

Boats C, E, F, G, H, and K are on port tack.

Boat A is in the process of tacking and is *not on a tack* until her sails have filled and she is under way.

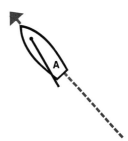

15-Q. When two boats meet on different tacks they must follow the Opposite Tack Rule.

This Fundamental Rule states that a port-tack boat shall keep clear of a starboard-tack boat (NAYRU Rule 36).

Boats A and B will collide unless one or both alter course.

☐   Boat A must tack at once.
☐   Boat B must tack at once.
☐   Boat B must fall off and pass below A's stern.
☐   Boat B may either tack or fall off.

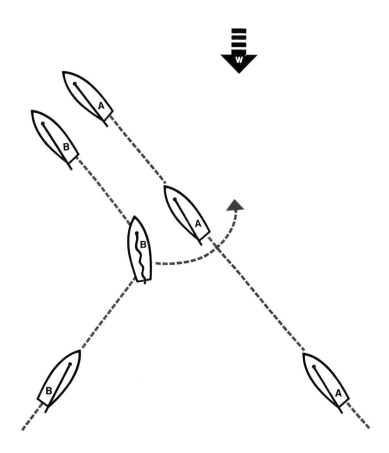

15-A. Boat B may *either* tack or fall off. She is the port-tack boat and must give right of way to Boat A on starboard tack. Any maneuver that keeps her clear of Boat A is permissible.

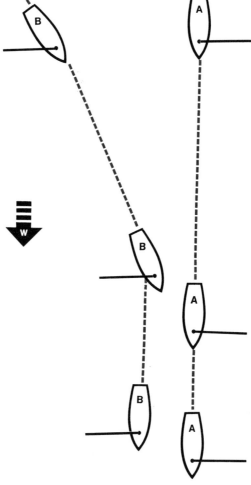

16-Q. Boats A and B are on converging courses on a run. Boat A does not alter her course, but Boat B does to avoid collision.

☐ Boat A is disqualified.

☐ Boat A has right of way under the Opposite Tack Rule.

☐ The Opposite Tack Rule does not apply here.

16-A. Boat A has right of way under the Opposite Tack Rule. Boat B is on port tack and must keep clear of the starboard-tack boat.

If Boat B were on a beat and on port tack, she would still have to keep clear of Boat A.

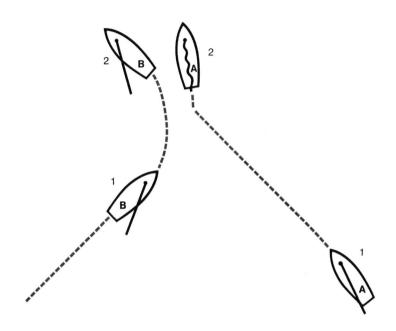

17-Q. Boat B is clearly ahead of Boat A when she decides to tack at point 1. By the time her tack is completed (point 2), Boat A has to head up sharply to avoid collision.

    ☐   Boat B is at fault for tacking too close.
    ☐   Boat B is at fault because she is on port tack.
    ☐   Boat A is at fault because no collision occurred.

17-A. Boat B is at fault, and is disqualified for tacking too close to Boat A.

    The "Tacking Too Close" Rule states that a boat which is either tacking or jibing shall keep clear of a boat on a tack (NAYRU Rule 41).

    Boat B tacked directly in front of A without allowing enough room to avoid a collision.

18-Q.   Since Boat B was well ahead of Boat A (Fig. 17-Q), why did they almost collide?

        ☐   Boat A was faster than Boat B.

        ☐   Boat B lost time and distance during her tacking maneuver.

18-A.   Boat B lost time and distance while tacking. Boats A and B are even at position 1, when B begins her tack. However, she loses two or three boat lengths in coming about.

Every boat loses speed when she tacks, because she must head up into the wind during this maneuver and loses her driving power when the sails luff. The racer must keep this loss of distance in mind when tacking in front of boats on the opposite tack.

The arc from B1 to B2 represents Boat B's "turning circle," the smallest circle in which the hull will turn for this wind.

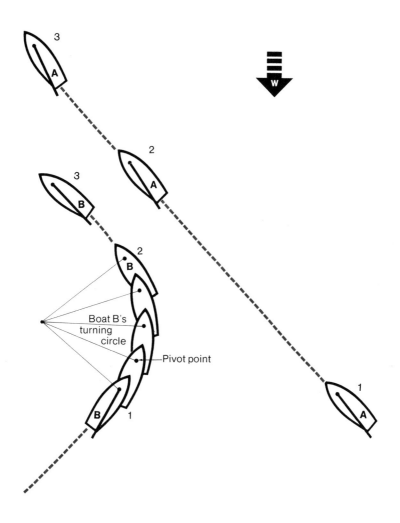

Boat B's
turning
circle

Pivot point

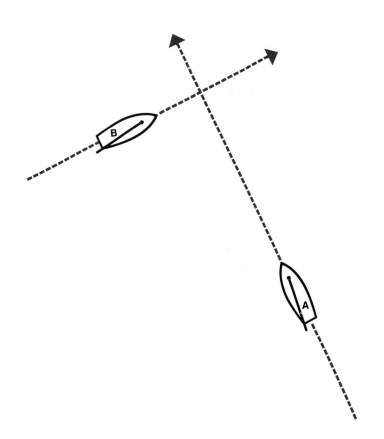

19-Q. Boat B, although on port tack, can safely cross Boat A's bow. What is her best competitive tactic to use, without fouling Boat A?

☐   Boat B crosses A's bow and tacks.
☐   Boat B crosses A's course and does not tack.

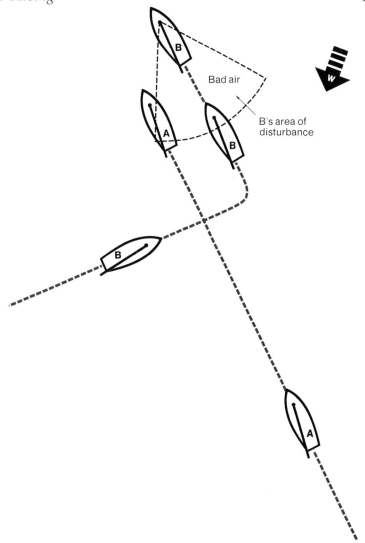

Bad air

B's area of
disturbance

19-A. Boat B crosses A's bow and tacks. In so doing, she loses ground to A, but not so much that she cannot blanket A effectively and give her bad air and rough wake to sail through.

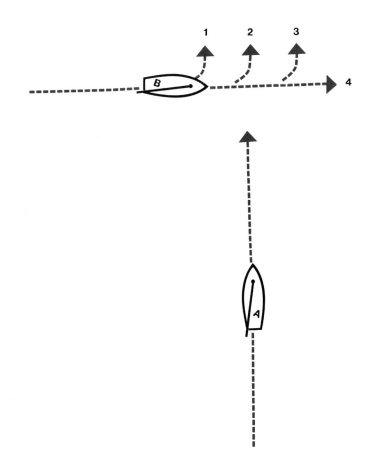

20-Q. Boat B is on port tack and well ahead. She is safely clear of Boat A.

However, she wants to effectively slow Boat A with backwind or blanketing. Where is the best and safest place to tack?

☐ Tack short of Boat A's course at point 1, or tack beyond it at point 3.
☐ Tack directly in front of Boat A at point 2.
☐ Don't tack (point 4).

Notice that Boat B is not as far ahead of Boat A as she was in the previous problem.

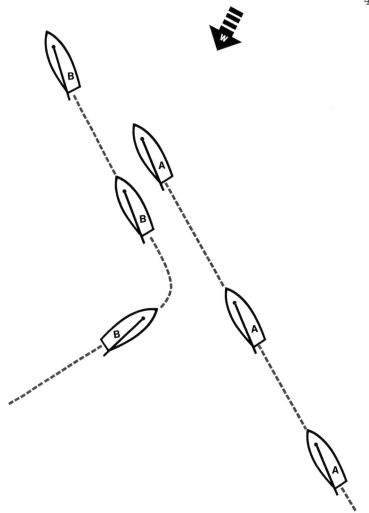

20-A. Tack short of Boat A's course at point 1, or tack beyond it at point 3.

Since there is loss of distance in coming about, tacking at point 2 is too risky because of danger of collision.

If Boat B tacks short of A's course, then hardens up to give Boat A backwind and wake, B will be securely ahead.

If, however, she chooses to tack at point 3, B will be in a position to blanket A, provided Boat A cannot sail ahead to a Safe Leeward Position.

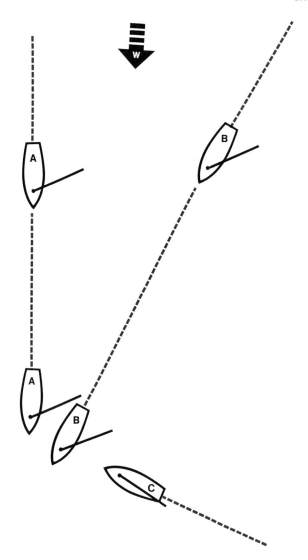

21-Q. Boats A, B, and C are on converging courses.

- ☐ Boat C must give way to Boats A and B.
- ☐ Boat A has right of way over both B and C.
- ☐ The Opposite Tack Rule does not apply here.

21-A. The Opposite Tack Rule does not apply here. All three boats are on the same tack.

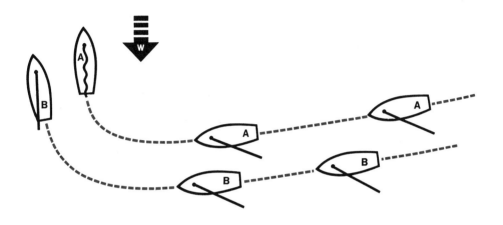

The Same Tack Rule, another Fundamental Rule, states in part that a windward boat shall keep clear of a leeward boat (NAYRU Rule 37.1).

Boat B is leeward of Boat A and can alter her course to windward. Boat A must do the same, even to the point of luffing.

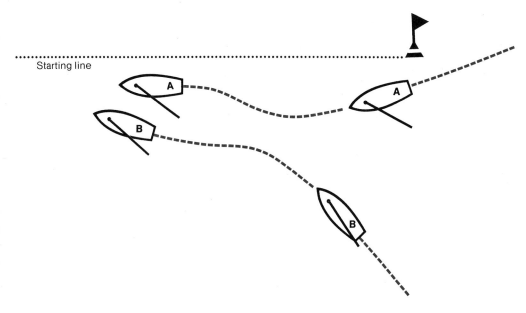

Starting line

22-Q. Before the start, Boat A, on a reach, bears down on Boat B, close-hauled, keeping her from the starting line.

☐ Boat A has the right of way because this is behind the starting line.

☐ Boat B has a good defense under the Same Tack Rule.

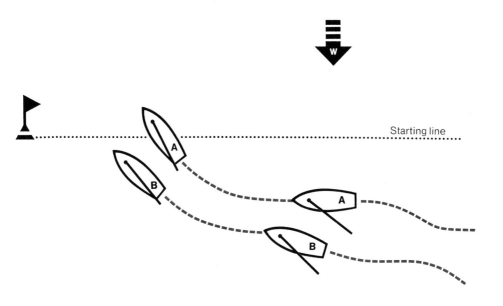

22-A. Boat B has a good defense under the Same Tack Rule.

It is common for windward boats to barge down on leeward boats at the start. The leeward boat can and should luff up any boats close above her, even to forcing them over the starting line early.

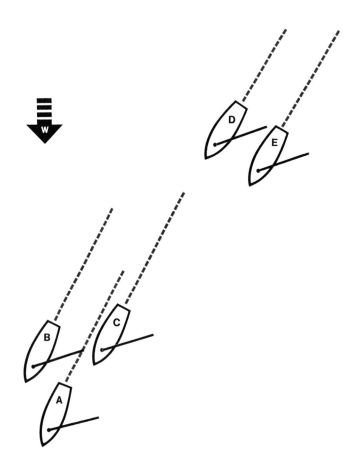

23-Q. On a broad reach, Boat A and Boat E are both in danger of being blanketed by windward boats.

    ☐   Only Boat E has a good defense.

    ☐   Boat E may luff Boat D, but Boat A may luff only Boat B.

    ☐   Boat E may luff Boat D, and Boat A may luff Boats B and C.

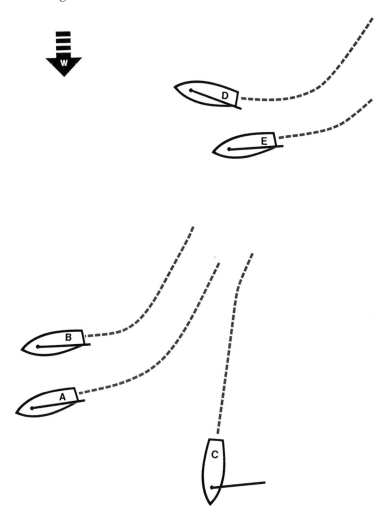

23-A. Boat E may luff Boat D, and Boat A may luff Boats B and C. Boat A is entitled to luff the boat that is clear astern as well as the windward boat. Boat C is probably far enough behind to keep clear of Boat A's stern.

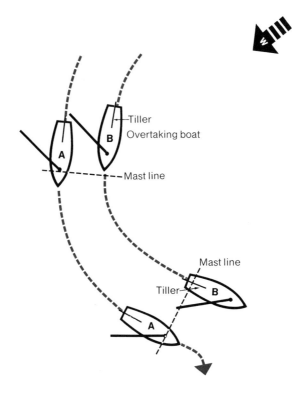

24-Q. Are there limitations as to when a leeward boat may luff the windward boat?

☐ She may always luff the windward boat, wherever she pleases.

☐ She must stop luffing when her "mast line" is abreast of or behind the windward boat's skipper.

24-A. The leeward boat (Boat A) has luffing rights only while a line drawn across from her mast is forward of the windward boat's helmsman (NAYRU Rule 38.1).

As soon as the skipper of Boat B comes abreast of or passes Boat A's "mast line," he may yell, "Mast abeam!" or words to that effect (NAYRU Rule 38.3), and the luffing must stop.

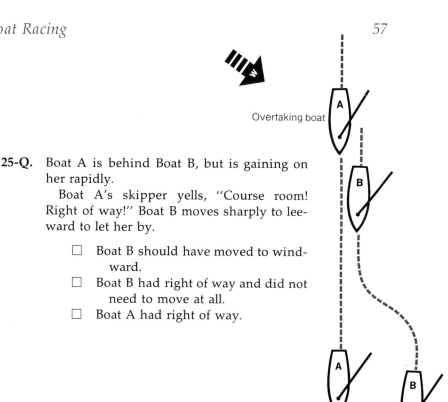

Overtaking boat

25-Q. Boat A is behind Boat B, but is gaining on her rapidly.

Boat A's skipper yells, "Course room! Right of way!" Boat B moves sharply to leeward to let her by.

☐ Boat B should have moved to windward.
☐ Boat B had right of way and did not need to move at all.
☐ Boat A had right of way.

25-A. Boat B had right of way and did not need to alter course. Under the Same Tack Rule, the boat behind must keep clear of any boat ahead (NAYRU Rule 37.2).

If Boat A is gaining, she must alter course either to windward or to leeward to avoid Boat B.

The yelling was probably only "psychological warfare."

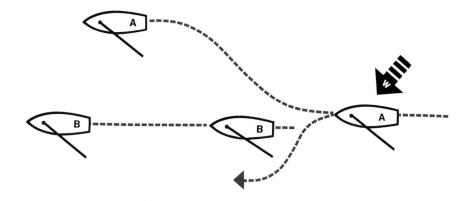

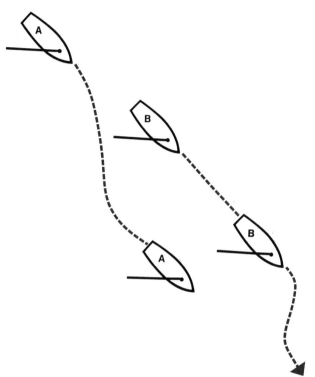

26-Q. Boat A, gaining on Boat B, does not want to be luffed above her course, so she falls off to pass to leeward.

   When A is within three boat lengths of B, Boat B falls off sharply to prevent her from passing.

☐ Boat B's move is illegal.
☐ Boat B's move is a good defensive maneuver to prevent Boat A from passing.

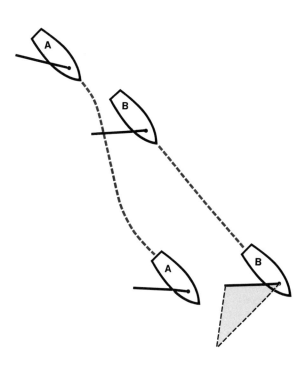

26-A. Boat B's move is illegal. On a reach or run, a boat may not fall off to leeward to prevent another from passing on her leeward side once that boat is within three boat lengths (NAYRU Rule 39).

Here Boat A falls below B and attempts to cut through the tip of her blanket zone to pass to leeward. Boat B may not move to stop her now. However, she could have fallen off before Boat A came within three boat lengths.

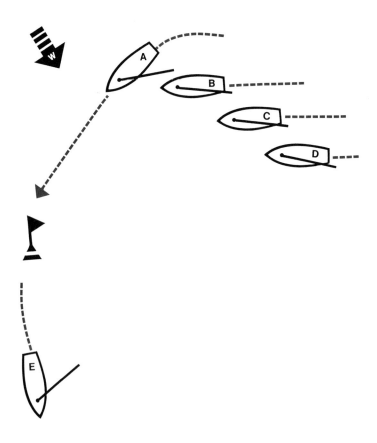

27-Q. Boat A is on the outside of Boat B. When near the weather
mark, she alters course to pass close to the mark.

Suddenly there are cries of "Buoy room!," "Room at
mark!," and "Right of way!" from the boats behind.

☐   Boat A is committing a foul.
☐   Boats B, C, and D are yelling only to confuse
     Boat A.
☐   At the mark, every boat is entitled to pass as
     closely as she can.

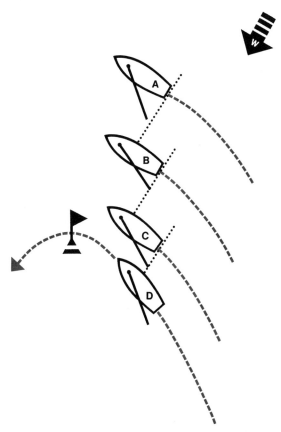

27-A. Boat A is committing a foul.

The "Buoy Room" Rule states that an outside boat must give room to each boat overlapping her on the inside at the mark (NAYRU Rule 42.1).

Boat D overlaps Boat C and is given room to round the mark. C in turn has an overlap on B and is allowed room. Since Boat B overlaps Boat A, A must give room to B, C, and D, and round on the outside.

28-Q. Boat A's position is a very poor one. Why?

☐   The outside is always bad at the mark.
☐   Boat A will not have clear wind after rounding.
☐   Boat A has had to sail farther.

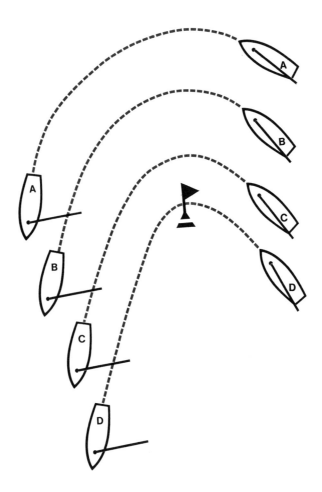

28-A. Boat A has had to sail farther. By the time all boats have gone around the mark, Boat A is still up to windward and behind.

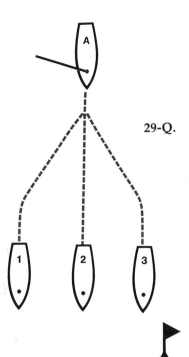

29-Q. Boat A approaches thc lccward mark alone. She wishes to pass the mark closely, as Boat B has done.

Her best course is:

☐ Swing wide to position 1.

☐ Steer a middle course to position 2.

☐ Move close to the mark before turning, at position 3.

29-A. Swing wide to position 1. By doing this she completes her rounding and is upweather of other boats, who are too close to the mark.

Boat C has tried to cut the turn too sharply and finds herself many boat lengths downwind.

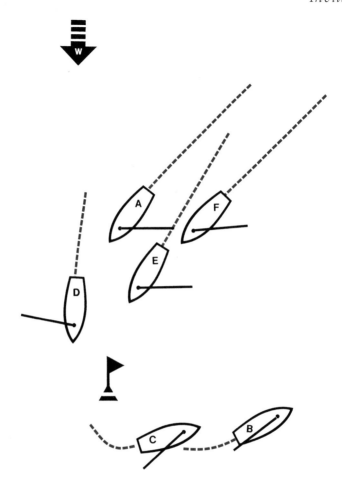

30-Q. Before the leeward mark is reached, Boat A makes sure she has an overlap on Boat E.
In this situation:

☐ Boat A cannot claim buoy room on Boat E.
☐ Boat F cannot claim buoy room on Boat A.
☐ Boat D is on port tack and cannot round in front of Boats A and E on starboard tack.

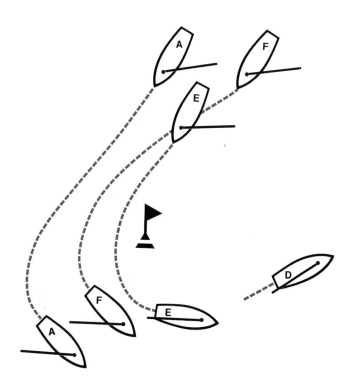

30-A. Boat A cannot claim buoy room on Boat E. Boat A has an overlap on Boat E, but it is on the *outside*. There is no way for E to give buoy room to A.

Boat F overlaps Boat A on the inside and must be allowed room to pass the mark.

Since Boat D was clear ahead as she began to round the mark, the "Buoy Room" Rule (NAYRU Rule 42.3[d]) takes precedence over the Opposite Tack Rule.

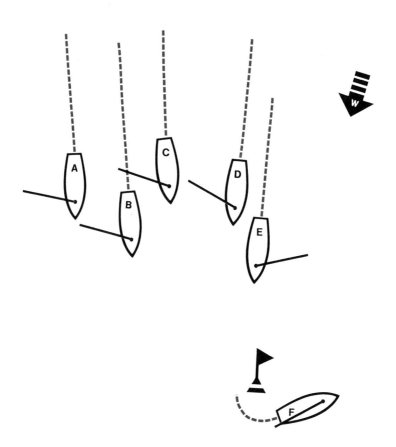

31-Q. In a moderate wind, Boat A finds herself on the outside of a group of boats approaching the leeward mark.

    ☐ Boat A's position is hopeless.
    ☐ Boat A can maneuver to the inside by first swinging to the outside.

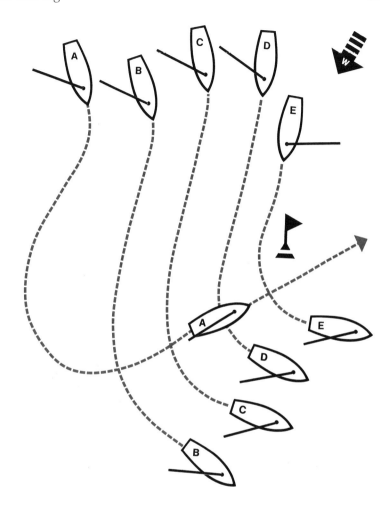

31-A. Boat A can maneuver to the inside by first swinging to the outside. By this means she effectively slows her speed and is able to cut behind the mass of boats rounding the mark. She completes her turn wide of the mark and passes it close, in good windward position.

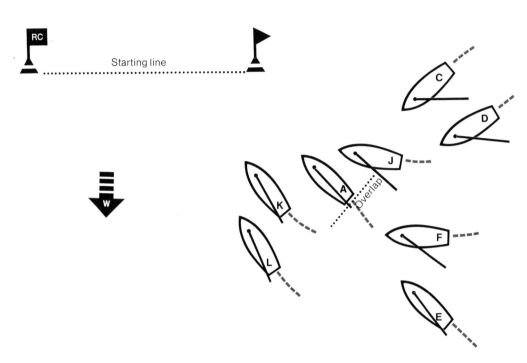

32-Q.   At the start, Boat A is overlapped by Boat J. Boat J yells for buoy room.

☐   Boat A is close-hauled and should fall off to make room.

☐   The "Buoy Room" Rule does not apply at the start.

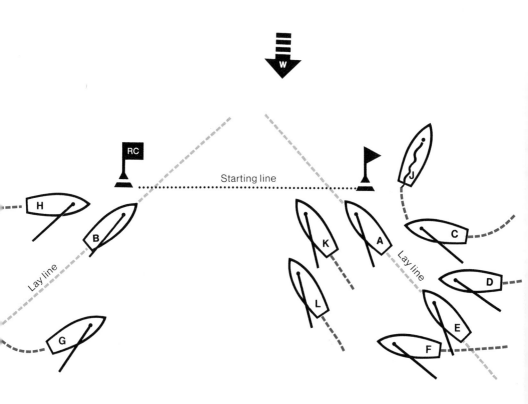

32-A. The "Buoy Room" Rule does not apply at the start.

The "Anti-Barging" Rule states that a leeward boat is under no obligation to give any windward boat buoy room at the start (NAYRU Rule 42.1[e]).

Boats A and B are both sailing on the lay line at opposite ends of the starting line. Even though overlapped, they do not have to give room at their marks. Boats H and J are badly out of position and must head up.

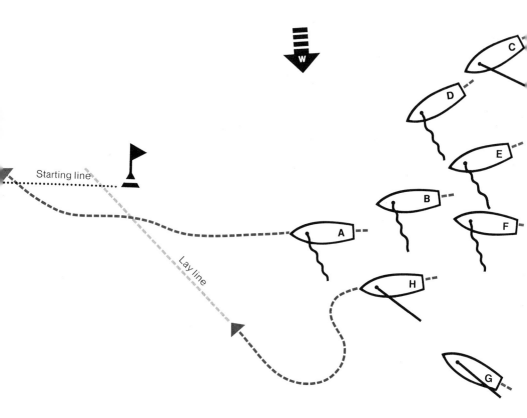

33-Q.   Most of the fleet are luffing because they are too early for
the start.

Boat A decides to luff her way down the starting line.
Boat H plans to fall off to leeward and approach on the
lay line.

Which boat has the more competitive start?

☐   Boat A.
☐   Boat H.
☐   Neither.

Which rules are involved?

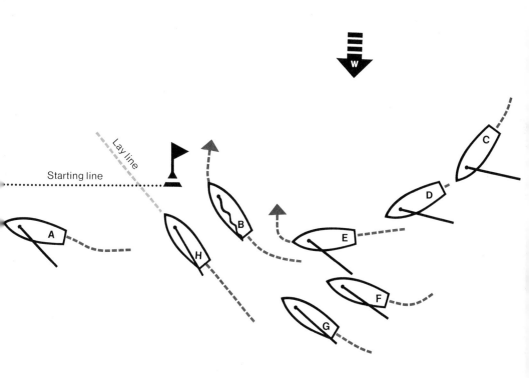

Starting line

Lay line

W

A B C D E F G H

33-A. Boat H has the more competitive start. She is using her right of way to hold back almost the whole fleet of barging boats. Theoretically, she will cross the starting line with good speed and in a favorable windward position. However, the crush of boats in most races prevents this.

Boat A's start is safe, and may be better, but reaching down the line is not recommended as a habit for starting.

The "Anti-Barging" Rule and the Same Tack Rule apply here.

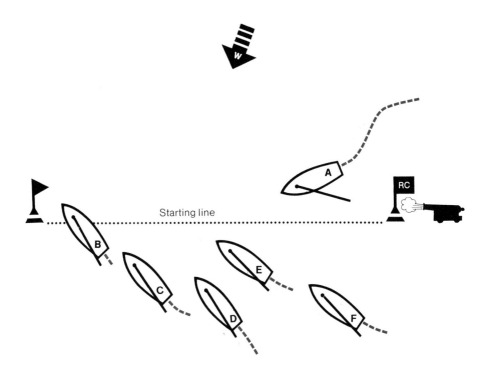

34-Q. The starting gun is just now signaling the start of the race.

☐ Boats A and B are disqualified.
☐ Boats A and B are disqualified but may restart.
☐ Boat A has right of way over boats behind the starting line.

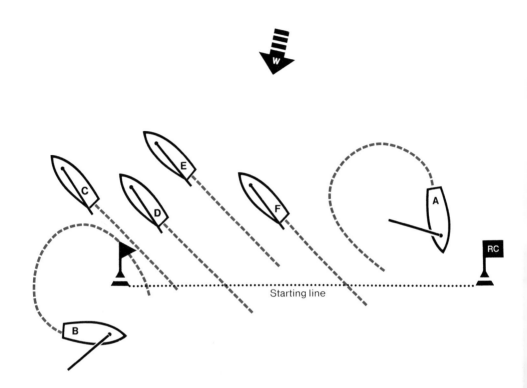

34-A. Boats A and B are disqualified but may restart.

The "Over Starting Line Early" Rule states that any boat on the wrong side of the starting line at the start has to keep clear of all other boats.

Boats A and B may restart after recrossing the starting line. Until they have done so, both must give right of way to all other boats, even those on port tack.

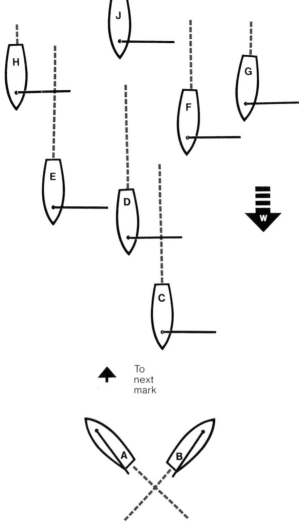

35-Q. Use the rules to plan your tactics.

Boats A and B split tacks halfway up the weather leg, only to see the boats ahead of them round the mark and start their run. Both will have to sail through this fleet of starboard-tack boats.

Boat A plans to sail a little farther, then tack and sail through the fleet on port tack. Boat B plans to come about after a short hitch and sail through the fleet on starboard.

Is there any advantage in the course chosen by either boat?

☐ No — both are equally bad.
☐ Boat A's course is better.
☐ Boat B's course is better.

What racing rules are involved?

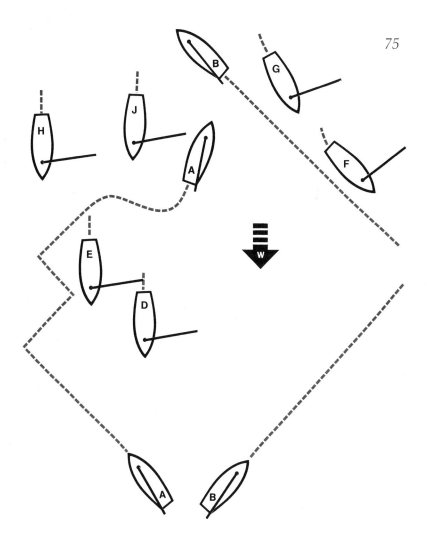

35-A. Boat B's course is better. Once they have tacked, Boat A will sail through the fleet on port tack, while Boat B sails through on starboard.

Since all the boats on the run are on starboard tack, this gives Boat B right of way under the Same Tack Rule, and the windward boats will make room for her.

Boat A is in trouble, as she is on port tack and under the Opposite Tack Rule must keep clear of the boats on the run. This costs her time, as she must tack to avoid them.

Strategy: When you see boats ahead that you must sail through, plan to be on a tack giving you right of way.

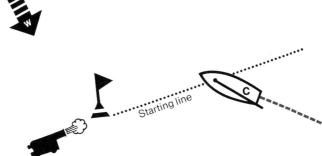

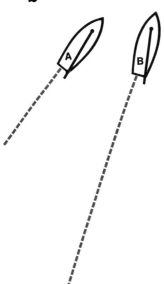

36-Q. Don't let your competitors bluff you!
"Room at the mark, I have an overlap!," shouts Boat A as the starting gun sounds.
"Leeward boat, right of way!," yells Boat B.
"Starboard tack!," hails Boat C.
Who really has the right of way?

☐ Only Boat A.
☐ Only Boat B.
☐ Only Boat C.
☐ Boats B and C have right of way over A.

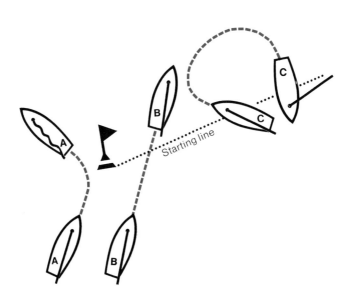

36-A. Boat B has right of way over both A and C. Boat C has no rights because she is over the starting line early. The Opposite Tack Rule does not apply. Boat A is barging; since she is not sailing on a close-hauled course, she may not claim buoy room from Boat B under the "Anti-Barging" Rule.

    Boats A and C must restart.

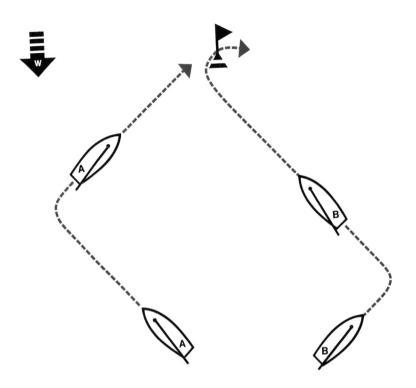

37-Q. Because of the Opposite Tack Rule, starboard tack is always preferred — or is it?

Boat A and Boat B approach the mark on opposite tacks and will pass it to starboard, as shown.

Whose approach is better?
    ☐   Boat A, on port tack.
    ☐   Boat B, on starboard tack.

What rules apply?

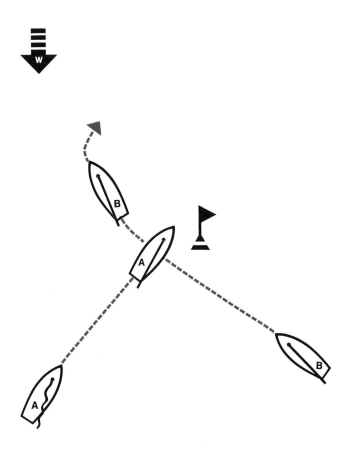

37-A. Boat A, on port tack, has the better approach. Boat B has to tack at the mark, but under the "Tacking Too Close" Rule she may not tack in front of A.

Boat A hails B and tells her to hold her course. Then, by luffing a little, she slows down enough to pass astern of Boat B, and fulfills her obligation to keep clear (Opposite Tack Rule).

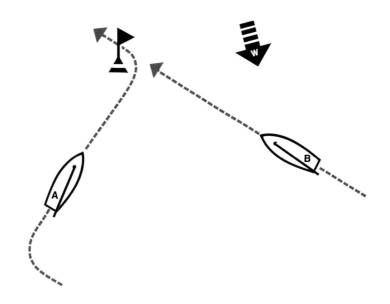

38-Q. If the marks are passed to port, does the port-tack boat still have the advantage?

☐ Boat A, on port tack, has the advantage.
☐ Boat B has the better approach because she does not have to tack at the mark.
☐ Boat B has the advantage only because of the Opposite Tack Rule.

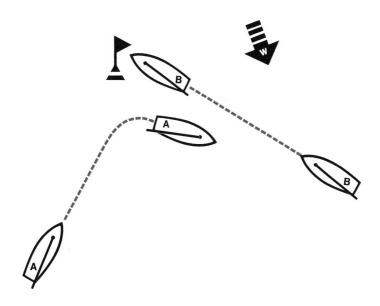

38-A. Boat B has the better approach because she does not have to tack at the mark. She also has some advantage because of the Opposite Tack Rule. By passing the mark with full headway she gains many boat lengths on A, who has to keep clear as well as tack.

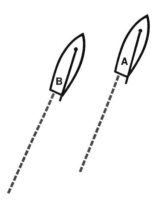

39-Q. What rules determine the tactics used if both boats have to tack at the mark?

In this common situation, Boats A and B will pass the mark to port, but each must tack to do so.

    ☐   Boat A may not tack until Boat B does, because of the "Tacking Too Close" Rule.

    ☐   Boat B has to tack as soon as she gets to the mark, because of the "Buoy Room" Rule.

    ☐   Boat A can tack at the mark and have right of way because of the Opposite Tack Rule.

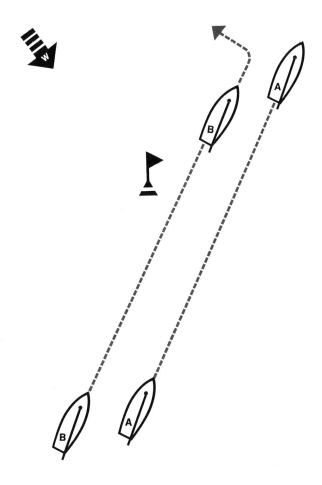

39-A. Boat A may not tack until Boat B does, because of the "Tacking Too Close" Rule (NAYRU Rule 41.2). Even though Boat A gives B a little backwind and pulls ahead, she must give buoy room and is still too close to tack safely.

Boat B uses this to her advantage and carries Boat A well beyond the mark, then tacks sharply, gaining a few boat lengths.

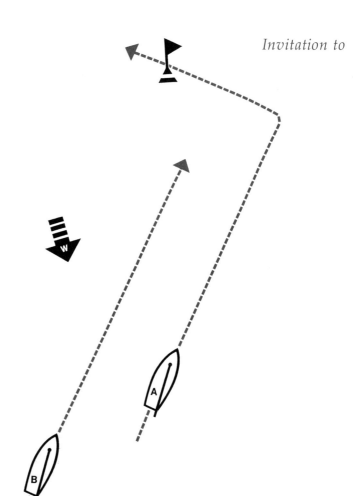

40-Q. Here Boat A is farther away from Boat B and farther
ahead. She plans to take a short tack on the lay line and
fetch the mark.

  ☐ Boat A is tacking too close.
  ☐ Since her sails will have filled on the new tack
    before she reaches the mark, she will have
    right of way under the Opposite Tack Rule.

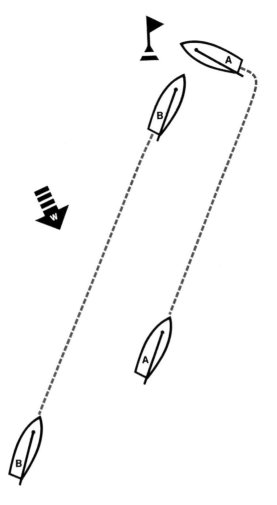

40-A. Boat A is tacking too close. Even though her sails have filled on the new tack, Boat A is directly in front of Boat B. Boat A has not allowed B enough time or distance to alter course to keep clear, which she now must do as the port-tack boat under the Opposite Tack Rule. Boat A is disqualified ("Tacking Too Close" Rule).

In this position Boat A has a difficult time beating Boat B around the mark, let alone avoiding being carried beyond the mark, as in Fig. 39-A.

Boat B's position (on Boat A's windward quarter) is a strong one, and is often used to keep a competitor from tacking.

There are ways for Boat A to get around B, depending on the distance between the boats and their relative positions. You should be familiar with these variations.

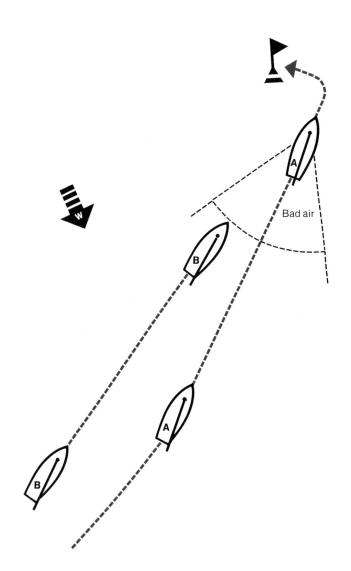

Bad air

41-Q. When Boat A is well ahead but her course is too close to
B's to permit her to tack (Figs. 40-Q and 40-A), then

    ☐ Boat A's best tactic is to pinch up and try to give
        B backwind.

    ☐ Boat A should try to luff Boat B to windward of
        the mark.

41-A. Boat A's best tactic is to pinch up and try to give Boat B
backwind.

    Pinching is the technique of tightening sheets and
sacrificing speed in order to point a few degrees higher.
Boat A will lose some distance while pinching, but the
gamble is worth taking. Once B is in her backwind, Boat
A will move ahead and can tack safely at the mark.

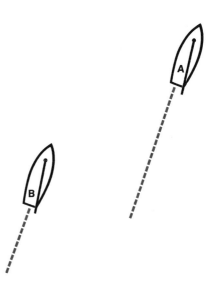

42-Q. If Boat A is farther ahead and her course is farther away than in Fig. 40-Q, she has another tactic she can use to beat Boat B around the mark.

☐ Boat A will hail Boat B, establish herself on starboard tack to round the mark and claim right of way.

☐ Boat A may not tack, because of the "Tacking Too Close" Rule, so will luff and slow down to pass Boat B.

☐ Boat A may claim right of way as leeward boat.

Show the course of both boats.

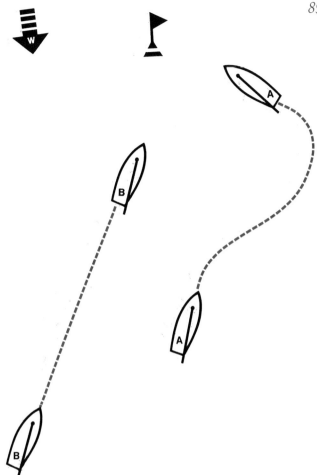

42-A. Boat A will hail Boat B, establish herself on starboard tack
and claim right of way. She hails B to warn her that she
is going to tack.

Η However, she first falls off to leeward to allow room to
complete her tack, which must be completed before Boat B
has to alter course to keep clear. Boat B passes astern of A,
who rounds the mark first on starboard tack.

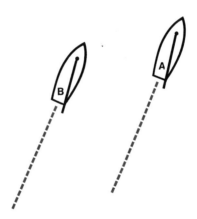

43-Q. If Boat A's course is the same distance from B's as in Fig. 42-Q, but she is not far enough ahead to tack and clear Boat B, can she use the same maneuver?

        ☐   Yes. (Show how.)
        ☐   No. (Why not?)

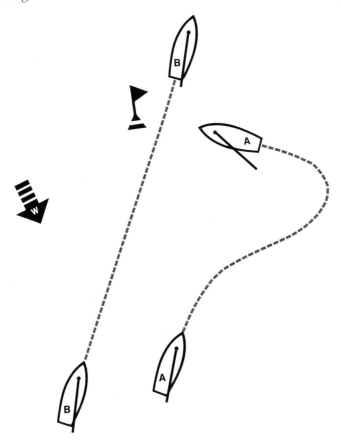

43-A. Yes. Boat A hails B to hold her course, then falls off to slow down, tacks onto starboard and passes under Boat B's stern. Boat B may not tack ("Tacking Too Close" Rule) until she is clear of Boat A, who rounds the mark first.

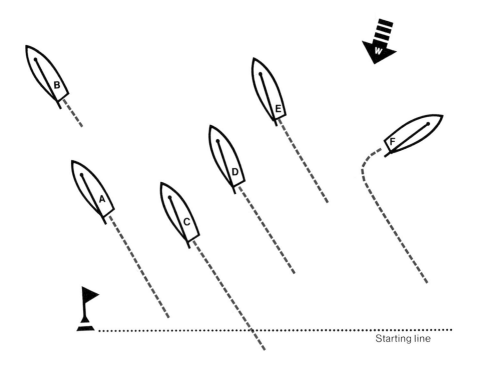

Starting line

44-Q. Apply these maneuvers and rules to your racing strategy. After the start, Boat E would like to prevent Boats A, B, C, and D from tacking into fresh wind, as Boat F is doing.

□ To do so, Boat E should stay on her present course.

□ Boat E will not have right of way over Boat B if B tacks.

□ Boat E should tack to give the others backwind.

Can Boat A tack?

□ Yes. (Show how.)

□ No. (Why not?)

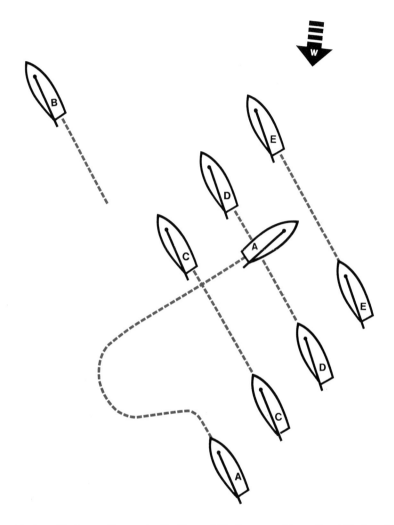

44-A. To keep Boats A, B, C, and D from tacking, Boat E should stay on her present course. Because of the "Tacking Too Close" Rule, the boats to leeward of E cannot tack safely until she does.

The one exception is Boat A. By first falling off, she is able to slow down enough to tack behind Boats C, D, and E and avoid backwind from Boat B. However, she sails through much turbulence before getting her wind clear.

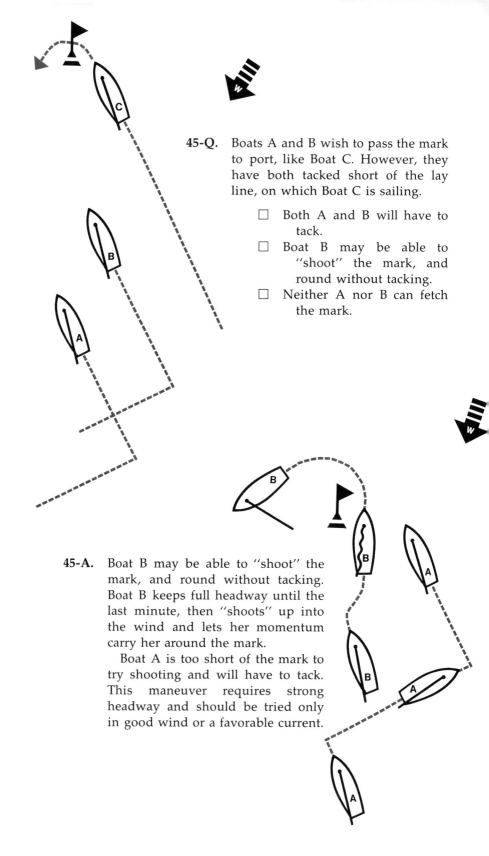

45-Q. Boats A and B wish to pass the mark to port, like Boat C. However, they have both tacked short of the lay line, on which Boat C is sailing.

- ☐ Both A and B will have to tack.
- ☐ Boat B may be able to "shoot" the mark, and round without tacking.
- ☐ Neither A nor B can fetch the mark.

45-A. Boat B may be able to "shoot" the mark, and round without tacking. Boat B keeps full headway until the last minute, then "shoots" up into the wind and lets her momentum carry her around the mark.

Boat A is too short of the mark to try shooting and will have to tack. This maneuver requires strong headway and should be tried only in good wind or a favorable current.

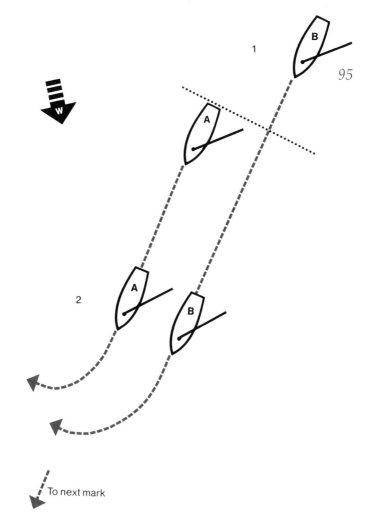

46-Q. With both boats on starboard tack and the next mark dead ahead, Boat B is clearly behind Boat A and is overtaking her to leeward (position 1).

She establishes an overlap, and with her mast line well forward of Boat A's skipper, she proceeds to luff Boat A to windward (position 2).

☐ Boat B may not luff Boat A.
☐ Boat B has luffing rights, under the Same Tack Rule.

46-A. Boat B may not luff Boat A. The Same Tack Rule states that a boat which establishes an overlap to leeward from a position clear astern shall not sail above her proper course (NAYRU Rule 37.3).

The proper course in this case is the one to the next mark.

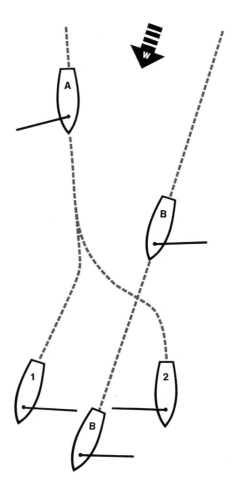

47-Q. Boat A, on port tack, is sailing a faster course and is overtaking Boat B, which is on starboard.

Boat A has two choices: (1) She could alter course by
jibing and remain on the windward side of Boat B. (2)
She could go astern of Boat B and pass to leeward with or
without jibing.

    ☐ Passing to windward is better.
    ☐ Going astern and passing to leeward is the
        better tactic.

(Read NAYRU Rule 38.2 before answering.)

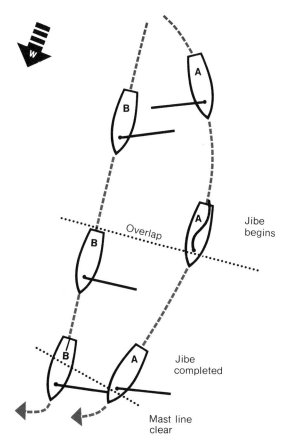

Jibe
begins

Overlap

Jibe
completed

Mast line
clear

47-A. Going astern and passing to leeward is the better tactic. This is because the Same Tack Rule (NAYRU Rule 38.2) states that an overlap begins when a tack or jibe is completed.

Boat A overlaps B to leeward with no right of way, since she is on port tack. By jibing, she begins a new overlap to leeward. Now, as long as her mast line is forward of Boat B's tiller, she has full luffing rights under the Same Tack Rule.

If Boat A had jibed and remained on the windward side of B, she would have become the overtaking boat as well as the windward boat and would have had to give right of way to B on both counts.

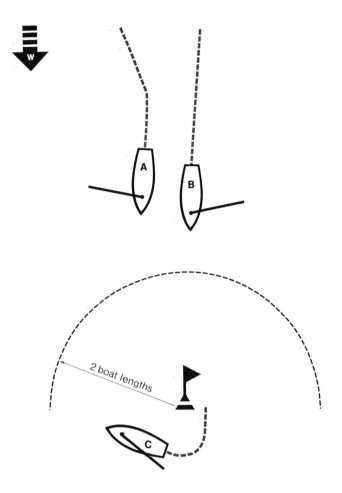

2 boat lengths

48-Q. Does a port-tack approach at the leeward mark make any difference?

Boat B, on starboard tack, is heading directly for the lee mark.

Boat A, as port-tack boat, alters course and has an overlap on Boat B. They are almost within two boat lengths of the mark.

☐ Boat B will have to give buoy room to A.

☐ Boat A cannot claim room at the mark because of the Opposite Tack Rule.

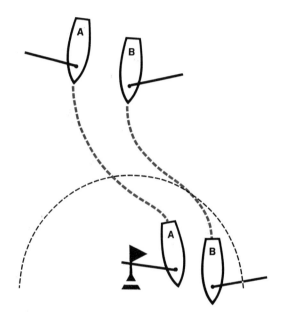

48-A. Boat B will have to give buoy room to A, since Boat A has established an overlap by the time they are two boat lengths from the mark. Starboard tack loses right of way in this situation, and the Opposite Tack Rule does not apply.

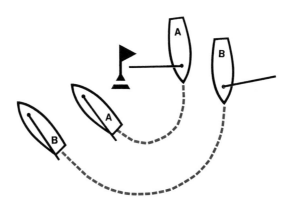

49-Q. How much room is "buoy room"?

☐ The outside boat must give the inside boat all the room she asks for.

☐ Buoy room is the width of one boat.

☐ Buoy room means enough room to round the mark without hitting it or another boat.

49-A. Buoy room means enough room to round the mark without hitting it or another boat.

At the leeward mark the inside position is preferred, because this boat becomes the windward boat for the next beat.

Nevertheless, there are ways to reduce the inside boat's advantage. The outside boat should force the inside boat to turn as tightly as possible, causing her to lose way and turn poorly.

Here Boat B allows A only enough room to clear the mark and complete her jibe. Boat A loses speed, and Boat B is able to gain a Safe Leeward Position.

50-Q. Why can't the outside boat swing wide and cut inside the other boat, as Boat B is doing here, gaining the windward position?

☐ Boat A won't let her.
☐ The "Buoy Room" Rule does not allow it.
☐ There is no reason not to, and it is an excellent maneuver.

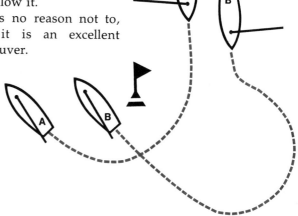

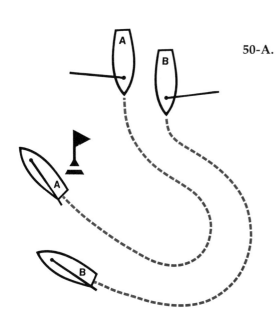

50-A. Boat A won't let her. As the outside boat (Boat B) swings wide, so does the inside boat (Boat A). She takes all the room given, and keeps Boat B on the outside and behind.

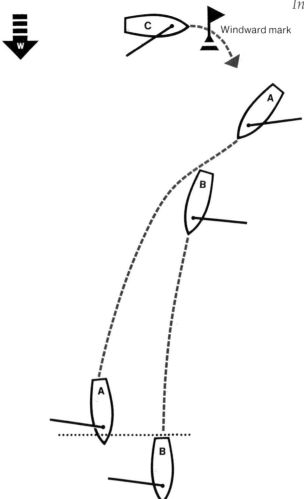

Windward mark

51-Q. Boat A wants to have buoy room at the next mark. As soon as she clears the windward mark, A moves early to be on the inside of Boat B.

☐ An overlap to leeward is a poor tactic.
☐ Boat A has made her move too soon.
☐ Boat B probably cannot break this overlap.

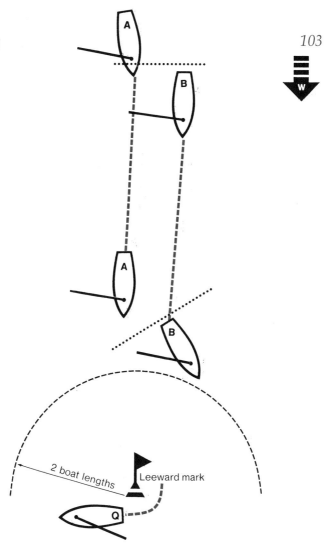

2 boat lengths Leeward mark

51-A. Boat A has made her move too soon. There are many ways to break an overlap, especially when it is a small one like this.

Just before they are two boat lengths from the mark, Boat B alters her course sharply to begin rounding. By doing this, she moves the line of her stern to break the overlap.

To be sure that Boat A has the message, B hails her before they reach the two-boat-length limit. Under NAYRU Rule 42.3(e)(ii), the outside boat has the responsibility for proving she was clear ahead before this limit is reached.

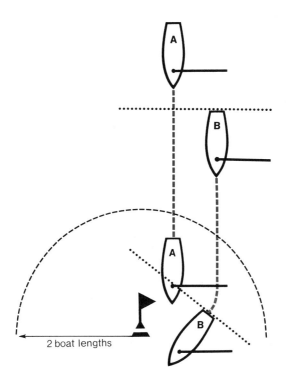

2 boat lengths

52-Q. Boat A does not have an overlap on Boat B when they are
two boat lengths from the mark. As Boat B begins to
swing around, the line of her stern also swings around,
giving Boat A an apparent overlap.

☐ Boat A can claim buoy room.
☐ Boat A has no right to buoy room and must keep
clear.

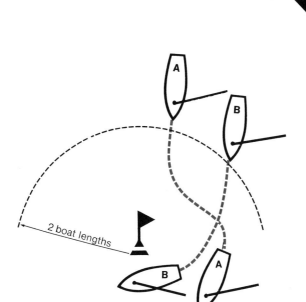

2 boat lengths

52-A. Boat A has no right to buoy room and must keep clear. She may do this by going astern of Boat B or going on the other side of the mark.

Under NAYRU Rule 42.3(a), an inside overlap must be established before the boats are within two boat lengths of the mark.

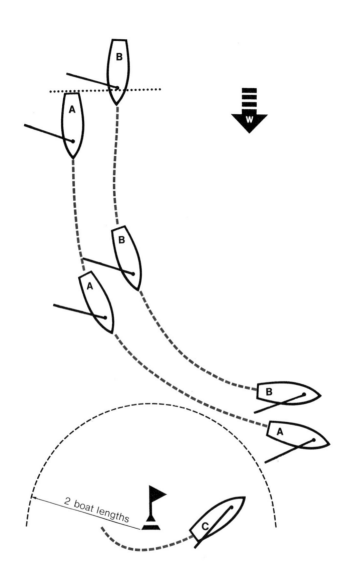

2 boat lengths

53-Q. You are on the Race Committee and have to decide a number of protests.

The first one involves Boat A, who was overlapped by Boat B well before the leeward mark.

"Buoy room!," yelled the skipper of Boat B.

"I have luffing rights, and I'm going to luff you so far from the mark you'll wish you'd never had buoy room," retorted Boat A.

Boat A then luffed Boat B to the wrong side of the mark and off the course. Boat B is protesting.

- ☐ Boat A's move was illegal and she should be disqualified.
- ☐ Boat B should be disqualified.
- ☐ Neither boat is disqualified.

53-A. Neither boat is disqualified. Boat A was within her rights.

NAYRU Rule 42.1(d) states that an outside leeward boat with luffing rights may take an inside boat to windward of a mark. She must hail to that effect and must luff before she is within two boat lengths of the mark, as well as passing to windward of it herself.

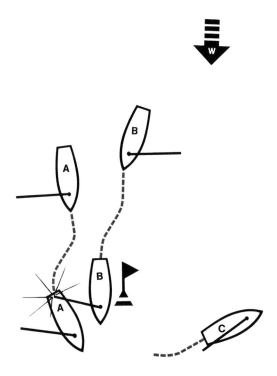

54-Q. As Race Committee Chairman, how would you decide this protest?

Boat B had an overlap on Boat A. The skipper of Boat B noticed that A was heading directly for the mark. He yelled, "Room at the mark!"

"I will give you all the room you need, fathead," growled the skipper of Boat A.

Boat B proceeded to jibe, and her boom hit the skipper of Boat A in an appropriate place.

"Deliberate foul!," skipper A cried, and protested.

☐ Boat B is disqualified.
☐ Boat A is disqualified.
☐ Neither boat is disqualified.

54-A. Boat A is disqualified. The "Buoy Room" Rule, NAYRU 42.1(a), states that buoy room includes room to tack or jibe when either is an integral part of the rounding or passing maneuver. Since Boat B approached the mark on starboard tack, she had to jibe in order to round the mark and should have been given room to do so.

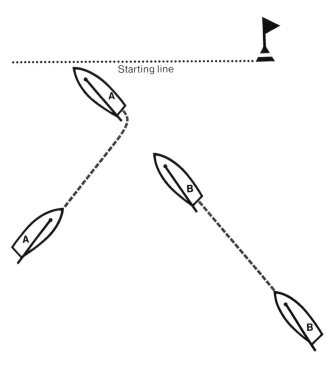

55-Q. How would you decide this protest?

Just before the start, Boat A, on port tack, came about directly in front of Boat B, on starboard tack. Boat B did not alter course until after the start, when she tacked to get clear of Boat A's backwind.

Because of this backwind, Boat B is protesting that Boat A tacked too close.

- ☐ Boat A is disqualified under the "Tacking Too Close" Rule.
- ☐ Boat A is disqualified under the Opposite Tack Rule.
- ☐ Boat A is disqualified for backwinding Boat B and making her tack.
- ☐ Boat A is not disqualified.

55-A. Boat A is not disqualified. Boat A tacked well ahead of Boat B, who did not have to change course to avoid collision. Boat A fulfilled her obligations under both the "Tacking Too Close" Rule and the Opposite Tack Rule. She may backwind as many boats as she wishes. Her maneuver to backwind Boat B at the start was good.

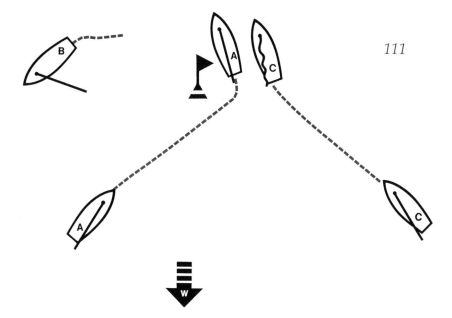

56-Q. Boat A is protesting Boat C for not giving her buoy room at the windward mark.

A and C were approaching the mark on opposite tacks, with Boat C slightly overstanding it. Boat A claims she had overlapped Boat C at the mark and was not given room to round. Boat C claims she had to alter course sharply and luff head-to-wind in order to avoid collision.

If you were on the Race Committee, what would be your ruling?

- ☐ Boat A is disqualified under the "Buoy Room" Rule.
- ☐ Boat A is disqualified under the Opposite Tack Rule.
- ☐ Boat C is disqualified under the "Buoy Room" Rule.
- ☐ Neither boat is disqualified.

56-A. Boat A is disqualified under the Opposite Tack Rule (NAYRU Rule 36).

At the windward mark (NAYRU Rule 42.1[c]), the Opposite Tack Rule takes precedence over the "Buoy Room" Rule—in contrast to what happens at the leeward mark.

Boat A's first obligation is to keep clear of the starboard-tack boat. If she could have completed her tack without causing Boat C to alter her course, then she might have been able to squeeze through at the mark.

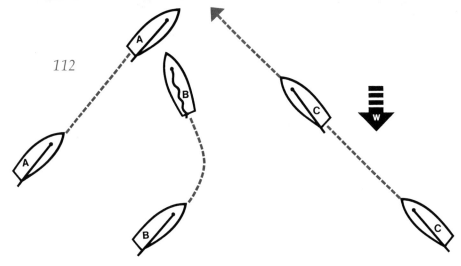

57-Q. This difficult protest involves a number of rules: the Opposite Tack Rule, the Same Tack Rule, the "Tacking Too Close" Rule, and the rule for Hailing for Room to Tack at Obstructions (NAYRU Rule 43).

Boats A and B were approaching the course of Boat C, who was on starboard tack. Boat A could safely cross C's bow, but Boat B could not. Boat B decided to tack, and because she felt Boat A was too close, she yelled over, "Room to tack, I have a starboard tack coming!"

"Go ahead and tack" was the reply from Boat A.

Boat B tacked, but collided with Boat A.

Boat B is protesting Boat A.

    ☐   Boat A is disqualified under the Responding provision of the Hailing for Room to Tack Rule (NAYRU Rule 43.2).

    ☐   Boat B is disqualified under the Opposite Tack Rule.

    ☐   Boat B is disqualified under the "Tacking Too Close" Rule.

57-A. Boat A is disqualified under the Responding provision (NAYRU Rule 43.2) of the Hailing for Room to Tack Rule.

This rule states that when two boats are on the same tack and the leeward boat must alter course to clear an obstruction, she may hail the windward boat for room to tack.

In this case Boat B hailed for room to tack and Boat A responded that she would have room. This put the burden on A, who should have kept clear by tacking. A right-of-way boat (Boat C) is considered an obstruction.

All the other rules mentioned have some place in this protest, but the Responding provision of the Hailing for Room to Tack Rule is the one violated.

58-Q. This protest is a simple one — or is it?

At the start, Boat C is over the starting line early, but does not know it because the Race Committee mark was hidden by Boat A's sail. C did not hear her number recalled; Boat B did, but she did not pass it on.

Shortly after the start, Boat B came about to port tack and demanded right of way over Boat C on starboard tack.

"You are out of it," Boat B yelled. "You were over the line early and have no rights."

Both boats had to alter course suddenly to prevent a collision, and then Boat C returned to the line and restarted.

☐   Boat B is disqualified for failing to give right of way to starboard-tack boat.

☐   Boat C is disqualified because she had no rights by reason of having been over the line before the start.

58-A. Boat B is disqualified for failing to give right of way to starboard-tack boat.

Part of the "Over Starting Line Early" Rule (NAYRU Rule 44.2) states that a premature starter shall be given all the rights under the rules until it becomes obvious that she is returning to restart.

Boat C was not returning to the line and was not even aware of having been over early, but still had right of way as starboard boat under the Opposite Tack Rule.

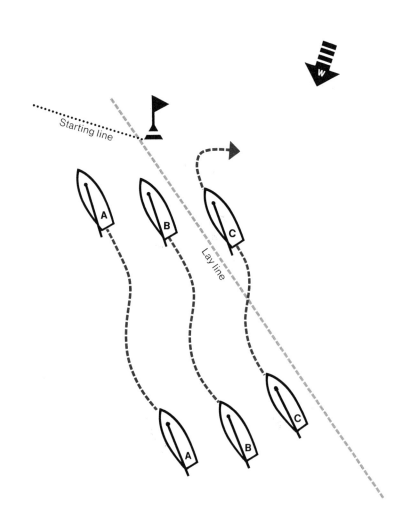

59-Q. Boat C is protesting Boats A and B for luffing her above the starting mark.

Prior to the start signal, Boat A, the leeward boat, luffed B. Boat B in turn luffed C above the lay line and held her there.

Boat C had an overlap, and demanded room at the mark. Neither Boat A nor Boat B would give way, B claiming she could not fall off because of A, and A claiming it was her right.

☐ Boat A is disqualified for not having had luffing rights on Boat C.

☐ Boats A and B are disqualified because they deprived Boat C of her place on the starting line.

☐ Boat B is disqualified under the "Buoy Room" Rule.

☐ No boat is disqualified.

59-A. No boat is disqualified. Before the start signal, a leeward boat may luff those boats to windward which she is entitled to luff under the Same Tack Rule, provided she does it slowly and gives them opportunity to respond and keep clear (NAYRU Rule 40).

Boat A had luffing rights on both B and C, which was necessary before she could luff C alone or B alone (NAYRU Rule 38.5).

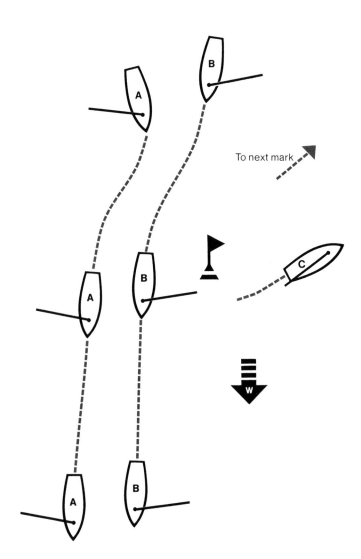

To next mark

60-Q. Would you sustain Boat A's protest or throw it out?

At the leeward mark, Boat B approached on starboard tack with right of way over port-tack Boat A, and established an overlap on A. In giving buoy room, Boat A also apparently gave some nautical invective to Boat B, free of charge.

"It's time to turn, buster," contributed A as they passed the flag.

"I'll round whenever I want to, needle-nose," retorted B as he kept on sailing beyond the mark, taking A with him.

Boat A is protesting Boat B under the "Buoy Room" Rule and claims B should have rounded the mark when they arrived at it. Boat B is defending herself with the Opposite Tack Rule, claiming she was within her rights as starboard-tack boat.

    ☐ Boat A's protest is upheld.
    ☐ Boat A's protest is thrown out since Boat B had right of way.

60-A. Boat A's protest is upheld.

Boat B did not jibe at the mark, which she is required to do by the "Buoy Room" Rule (NAYRU Rule 42.1[b]).

The point here is that the inside boat must jibe at the leeward mark and cannot claim right of way as an opposite-tack boat even if she is on starboard tack. At the windward mark the converse is true, and the Opposite Tack Rule has precedence over the "Buoy Room" Rule.

PART III

Racing Against the Local Fleet
Gaining Clear Wind
Playing Wind Shifts
Choosing Where to Start
Common Problems Encountered
over the Course

In this section, the various common problems are presented that every sailor faces in a race. However, all racing skippers should be prepared for the unexpected, so some more intricate problems are intermingled with the everyday ones for variety.

Throughout Part III the reader is put into Boat A as skipper, and is asked to solve tactical problems or to plan strategy for events lying ahead.

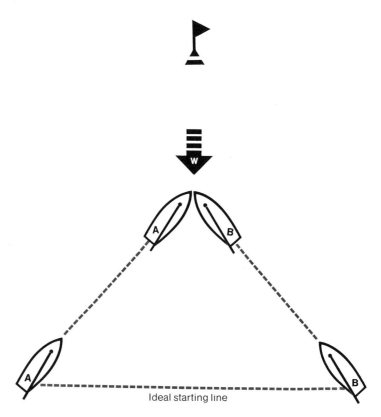

Ideal starting line

61. The first decision you make in a race is where to start on the line. Then you determine how to get there, which tack to be on, and how to time it.

Often one end of the line is favored by being closer to the wind or to the next mark, and it is to your advantage to start there.

For this reason, the race Committee tries to set an ideal starting line at right angles to the wind and to the weather mark. In this situation, two boats on opposite tack from the opposite ends of the line will sail the same distance before they meet, and will sail the same distance to the mark.

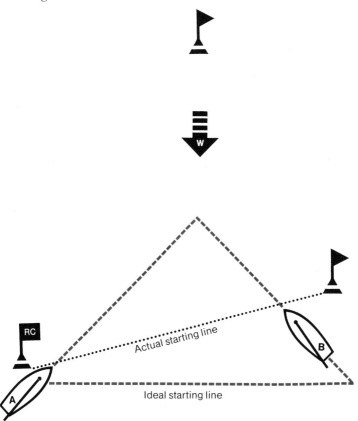

Actual starting line

Ideal starting line

62. If the Race Committee sets the starting line with one end nearer the wind, the boat on that end has less distance to sail. Here Boat B is already ahead of Boat A, because from her end of the line she will have a shorter distance to sail to meet Boat A.

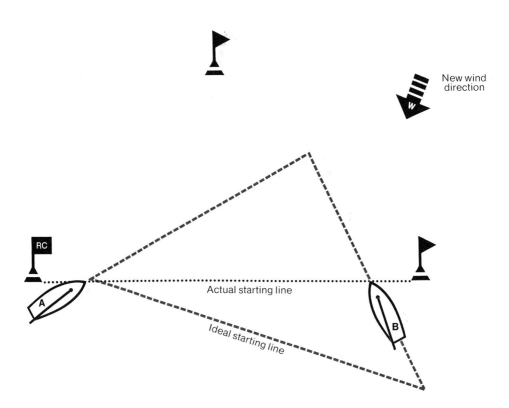

New wind
direction

RC

Actual starting line

Ideal starting line

A

B

63. If the line is square to the next mark but the wind shifts, the effect is the same. Here the new wind shift moves the whole wind triangle and again puts Boat B ahead of Boat A on the starting line.

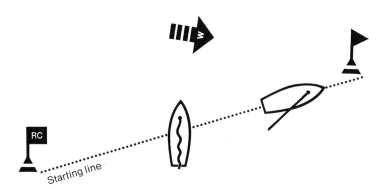

64-Q. How can you tell which end of the starting line is moved to windward?

☐ Luff up head-to-wind in the middle of the line and sight down both ends of the line.

☐ Reach back and forth along the line a few times.

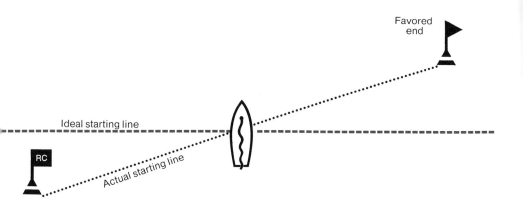

64-A. Luff up head-to-wind in the middle of the line and sight down both ends of the line. If one end of the starting line is forward of your beam, then that end is favored.

Reaching along the starting line, a common practice among beginners, is totally unreliable as a means of finding wind direction or the favored end.

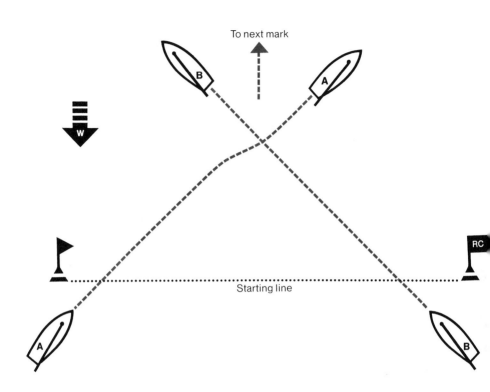

65-Q. Here the starting line is square to the wind and square to the next mark, so neither end is favored.

Except for what ground she loses giving right of way, a boat on port tack from the leeward end of the line is essentially even with the boat on starboard tack from the windward end of the line.

☐ This means a port-tack start is as safe as a starboard-tack start.

☐ This means a port-tack start is advisable only when there are not many boats on starboard tack claiming right of way.

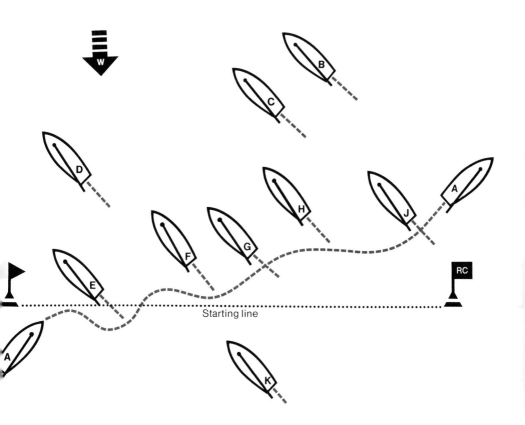

65-A. A port-tack start is advisable only when there are not many boats on starboard tack claiming right of way.

Here Boat A has a whole line of starboard-tack boats to contend with, and loses ground giving each one right of way. She goes under most of them, across the bow of one, and is lucky to start in ninth place.

There may be many good reasons for her to be on port tack at the start, but facing all starboard-tack boats on a crowded line is foolish.

A quick tack at the leeward mark and bearing off under Boat E would have been better, and would have averted sailing through the disturbed air from all the starboard-tack boats.

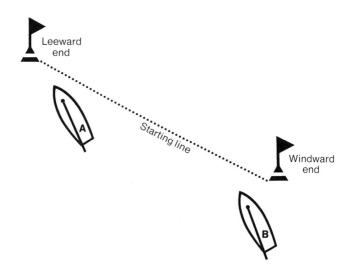

66-Q. Here the wind is blowing directly from the weather mark toward the starting line. However, the line is not square to the first leg of the course.

    ☐ The leeward end is favored.
    ☐ The windward end is favored.
    ☐ Because of the wind, neither end is favored.

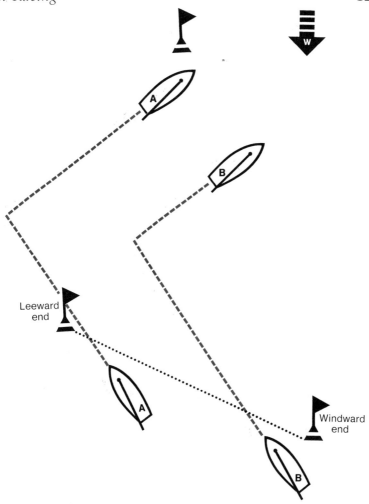

66-A. The leeward end is favored. This end is nearer the weather mark, and a boat starting here simply has less distance to travel.

When Boat A, who starts at the leeward end, has sailed the same distance as Boat B, she is well ahead of B, who started at the windward end.

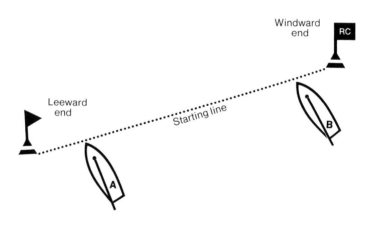

67-Q. The Race Committee has moved the starting line because the leeward end had too much advantage. Five minutes before your start, the wind shifts 30 degrees to the east.

☐ The wind shift makes the windward end the place to start.

☐ The leeward end is still favored because of the shift.

☐ Neither end is favored, because both are the same distance from the weather mark.

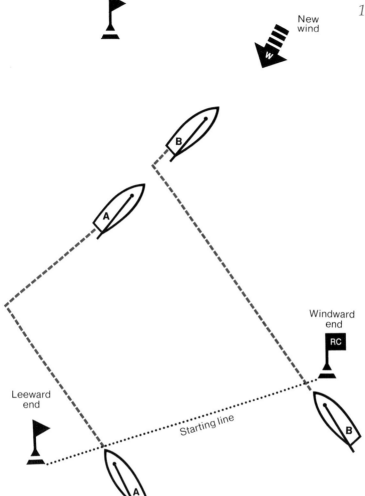

New wind

Windward end

RC

Leeward end

Starting line

67-A. The wind shift makes the windward end the place to start.

The new wind allows Boat B, at the windward end, to nearly lay the mark. Starting at the other end, Boat A is behind immediately, because she has to make up the distance to windward that Boat B gained at the start.

Boat B easily puts A in her backwind. Compare their courses here with those in Fig. 66-A.

New wind

Leeward end   Windward end

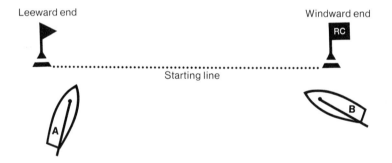

Starting line

68-Q. Here you are as Boat A on a port-tack start.

☐ Good choice; the leeward end is favored.
☐ Bad choice; the windward end is favored.
☐ Bad choice; Boat B will take you on starboard
    tack.

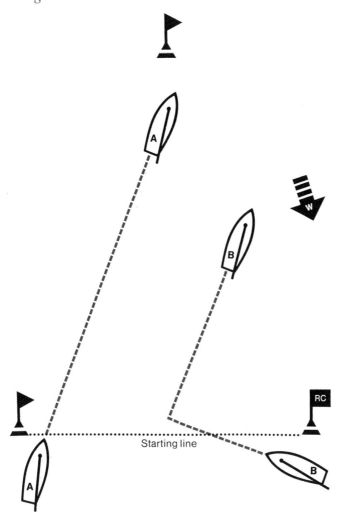

Starting line

68-A. Good choice; the leeward end is favored. Because of the wind shift, Boat B is lucky to cross the line at all on starboard tack. You are ahead right from the start.

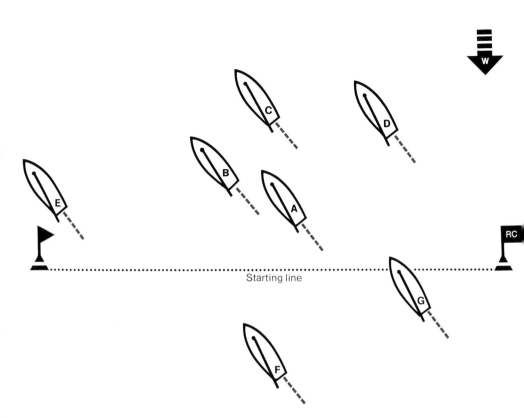

69-Q. Neither end was favored, so you (Boat A) have started near the middle of the line.

Unfortunately, your boat does not seem to be moving well. She is slow and feels sluggish. The most likely reason is:

☐ You have the wrong sails for this wind.
☐ Poor position.
☐ Kelp or seaweed is probably caught on your rudder.

What can you do about it?

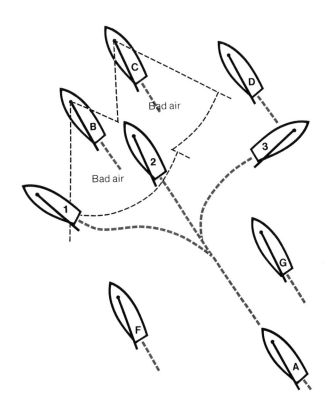

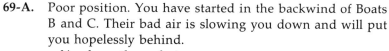

69-A. Poor position. You have started in the backwind of Boats B and C. Their bad air is slowing you down and will put you hopelessly behind.

  You have three choices:

1. Fall off on a faster course and try to break through the bad air to leeward. However, this may put you in Boat E's backwind, so it is not the best maneuver.

2. Remain where you are and hope B and C will tack. This is useless.

3. Tack at once, if you can find an opening between the starboard-tack boats, and get your wind clear. This is your best tactic.

  Don't blame the sails or seaweed because you are going slowly in bad air. Get out!

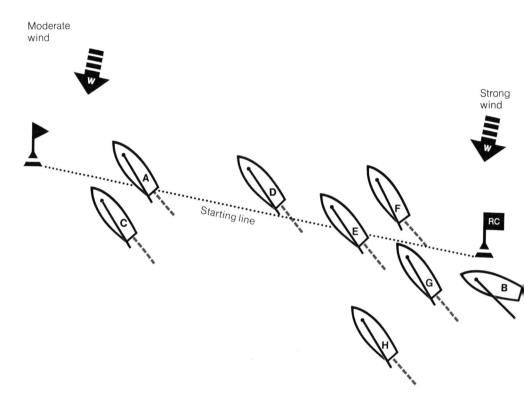

70-Q. This time you plan to be more careful and to have a truly
magnificent start.

As Boat A, you cross the line near the leeward end, because it is closer to the wind and the next mark. Your
wind is clear and no boat is giving you bad air.

Before the start you noticed that the wind was stronger
on the starboard side of the course, so you plan to work
over that way on this leg.

☐   This is a truly magnificent start.
☐   This is a poor start; you're on the wrong end.
☐   Boat D has the best start.

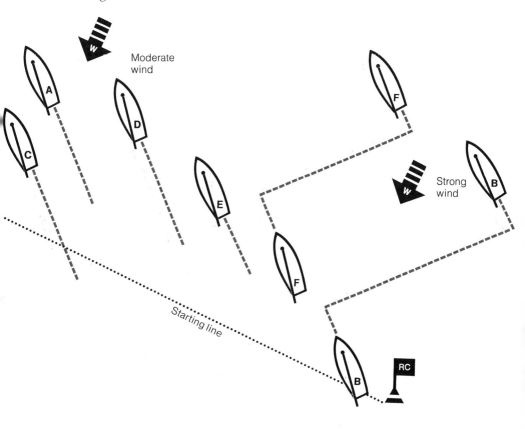

70-A. This is a poor start; you're on the wrong end.

Why? Because the boats on the other end can tack immediately into the new wind. Boat F and even Boat B, who had a late barging start, tack into the strong wind and work out insurmountable leads. You are boxed in by Boats C and D and cannot tack.

You had planned to sail in this wind on the first leg of the course, but you did not pay attention to how to get there. This should have been the most important factor in deciding where on the line you would start.

Always arrange your starts around the plan for the first leg.

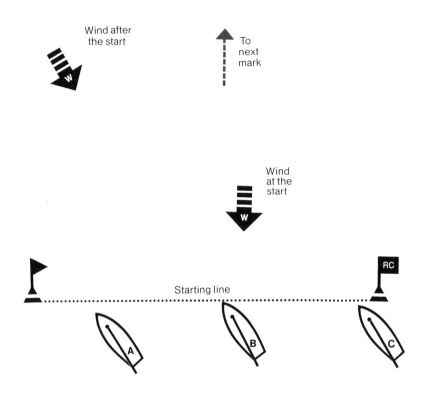

71-Q. It is often difficult to plan the first leg of your course in advance. One of the commonest factors is a wind shift, and knowing how to use it.

In this race, you know the wind will shift farther along the course. Which boat, if any, will benefit by this shift?

☐ Boat A will benefit most.
☐ Boat C will benefit most.
☐ No one will benefit, because all boats will have the same shift.

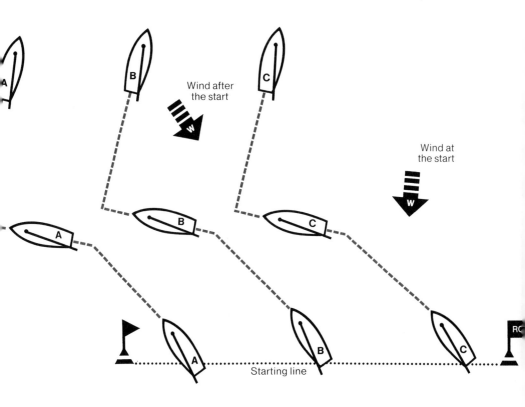

71-A. Boat A will benefit most.

The new wind heads the boats so that they are almost one behind another on starboard tack. Boat A backwinds B, who backwinds C.

When they tack, Boat A is much farther upwind than the other two, who have no chance of catching her unless the wind shifts back.

On this starting line, the leeward end was favored.

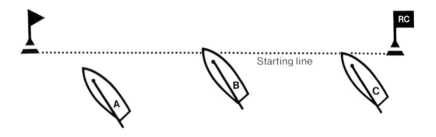

72-Q.   Here the predicted wind shift is 30 degrees to the east, shortly after the start.

☐   Boat A will gain the most.
☐   Boat C will gain the most.
☐   Boat C will gain the most but will have to tack first.

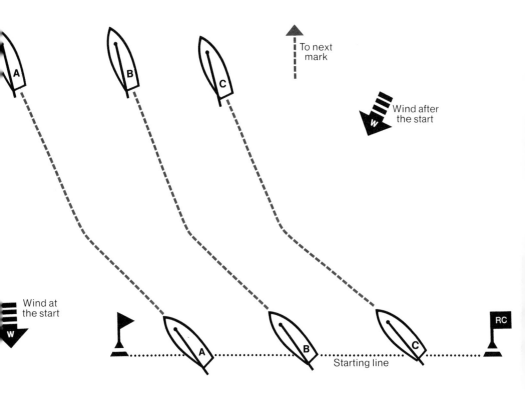

72-A. Boat C will gain the most. This wind shift is a "lift," and allows all the boats to point higher. Since Boat C is on the windward side of Boats A and B to begin with, the change of direction puts her more upwind and closer to the next mark.

The windward end of this starting line was favored.

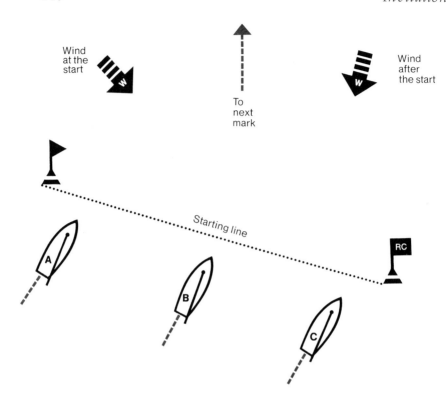

73-Q. These three boats are starting on port tack in a wind shift. The wind is expected, however, to shift back soon.

At the start, which boat has the most advantage from the wind?

☐   Boat A.
☐   Boat B.
☐   Boat C.

When the wind changes, the three boats will be:

☐   "Lifted."
☐   "Headed."

Who will have the advantage when the wind changes?

☐   Boat A.
☐   Boat C.
☐   No one.

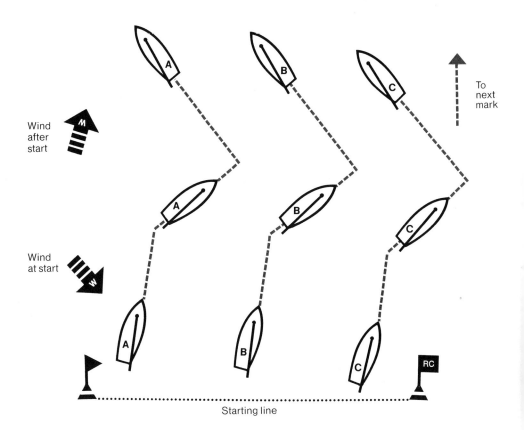

73-A. Boat A has the advantage at the start. In fact, she is ahead of Boat C by almost the length of the starting line.

When the wind reverts to normal, the boats are "headed"—that is, the wind is coming nearly over their bows, and they must fall off in order to maintain headway.

All three boats tack in the header. Boat A's advantage disappears, because the wind is now perpendicular to the starting line.

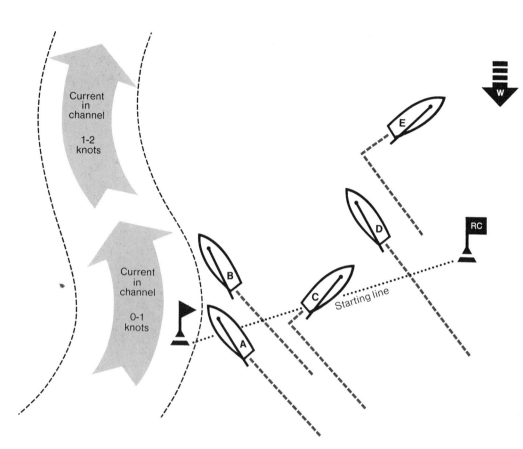

74-Q. In this race, the wind and line favor the windward end. However, you (Boat A) have decided to sail up the port side of the course, and so have started on the leeward end.

Interference from Boats B and C has forced you to be late to the line.

☐ Boat E has the best start; you are too late.
☐ You will probably beat Boat E to the next mark.
☐ You should flop over onto port tack as soon as possible.

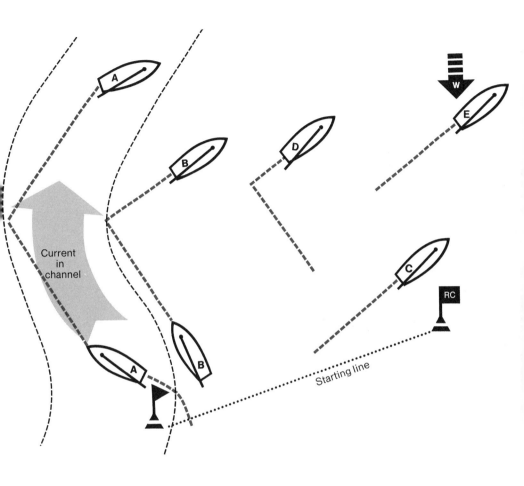

74-A. You will probably beat Boat E to the next mark.

    You have followed a good plan and sailed up the port side of the course, where you are moved up to windward by the strong current in the channel. With the rest of the fleet tacking away from this favoring current, you will soon have a commanding lead.

    Boat B was no problem. You simply fell off to leeward and broke through her backwind.

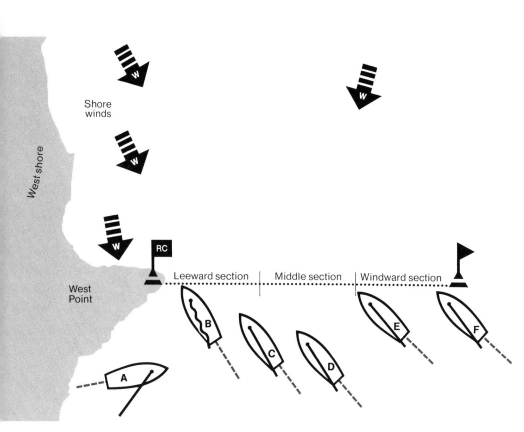

75-Q. This starting line is run from shore, but the water is fully navigable. In which section would you choose to start?

    ☐ Leeward section.
    ☐ Middle section.
    ☐ Windward section.

What was the most important reason for your choice?

    ☐ Ability to tack quickly.
    ☐ Clear wind ahead.
    ☐ The shore winds.
    ☐ Fewer boats on the line.

75-A. The leeward section is preferred, so that you can sail into the westerly shore winds as soon as possible. These will head you, but when you flop over onto port tack you will have a nice lift.

There is some risk in starting too far to leeward, since if you are early there is no place to go. A start in the middle section would be safer. But the boat that uses the shore winds first will probably work out a long lead.

The shore winds, however, are not always westerly; they vary with the geography of the area—so find out!

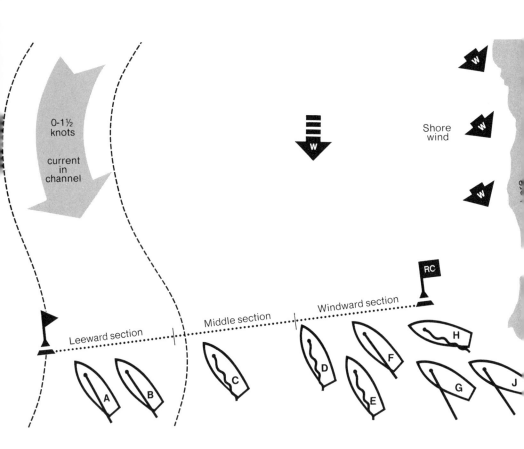

76-Q. Study this situation carefully. There are many boats crowding the starting line. Some are early and luffing; others are barging. Some want to play the east shore, while others will go west.

Where on the line would you start?

☐ Leeward section.
☐ Middle section.
☐ Windward section.

What was your most important reason for choosing this start?

☐ You planned to sail in the current.
☐ You planned to sail up the middle of the course.
☐ You planned to sail into the shore wind on the east.
☐ There were fewer boats in that section.
☐ There were more boats there than anywhere else.

76-A. The middle section is your choice, because you planned to sail up the middle of the course.

The leeward section is out because the tide has turned and now the current is going against you.

Not only is the windward end jammed with boats, which makes any start there a poor bet, but the shore winds are not of benefit. They will provide a lift, but this helps only the boats nearer the center of the course, not those near the shore.

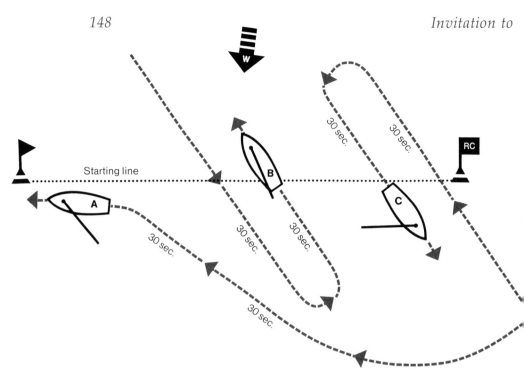

77-Q. Once you have picked where you want to start on the line, the next problem is timing your approach so that you arrive there with the starting signal.

Boat A shows one method of doing this. She plans to start on starboard tack at the leeward end, so she approaches the line from below on a long reach.

Boats B and C use the method of sailing close-hauled across the line, spending one minute above the line and one minute below. They time it so that the last 30 seconds are spent on the final tack for the line. This method gives them a good idea of any wind shifts before the start.

In this race there is only one minute to go before the start. Assuming the boats will continue at the same rate of speed for that last 60 seconds, which one has the best-timed start?

☐ Boat A.
☐ Boat B.
☐ Boat C.

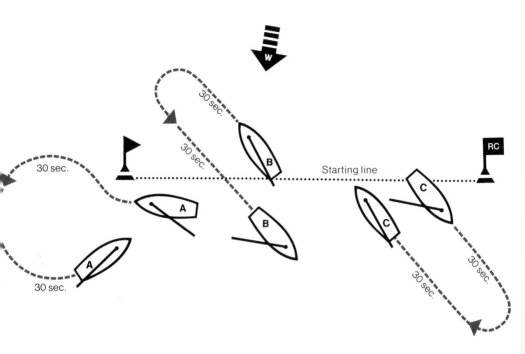

77-A. Boat C has the best-timed start. Boat B is going the wrong way at the start, and Boat A was too early at the leeward mark with no place to go. This is one of the dangers of trying to start in "Coffin Corner."

Strategy: Be on the proper side of the line during the last minute before your start.

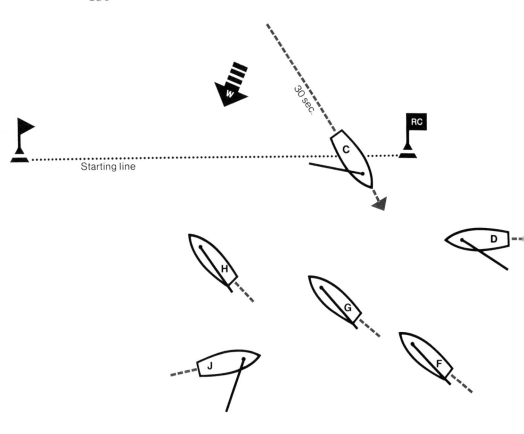

78-Q. Boat C's start (Fig. 77-A) was well timed, but there were no other boats near enough to interfere.

With other boats jockeying for position before the start, what will be the effect of the ensuing chop and disturbed air on C's timing?

☐ None. They will affect her equally going away from the line and going to it.

☐ She should allow more time to return to the line—say, 20 seconds down and 40 seconds back up.

☐ She will need more time down—say, 40 seconds—for more maneuvering.

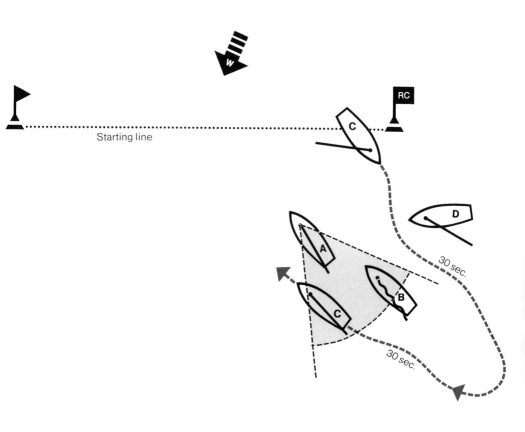

78-A. She should allow more time to return to the line — say, 20 seconds down and 40 seconds back up.

Here Boat C did not allow extra time for her return and is trapped well below the line because her speed is sharply reduced by the wind and wake from the other boats.

Strategy: Give yourself extra time for the final approach: allow for bad air and wake.

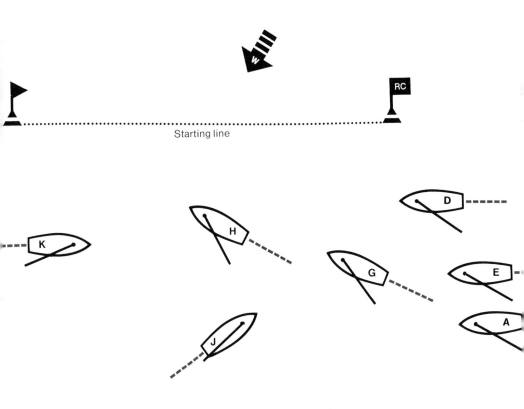

Starting line

79-Q.   What about Boat A? In Figs. 77-Q and 77-A, her long
reaching start was too early. What will happen now that
more boats are in the starting area?

☐   More boats will make her start worse.
☐   Her timing will allow for the interference of
other boats.

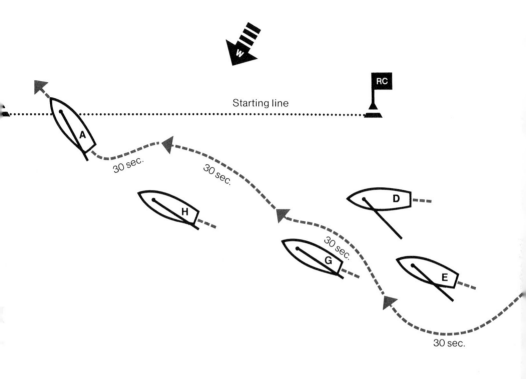

79-A. Her timing will allow for the interference of other boats. Boat A is able to use up all her extra time in avoiding other boats and being slowed down by the disturbed air and water.

This is a good start—but it would be safer if she did not try for the very end of the line.

Strategy: Avoid starting on the extreme ends of the line.

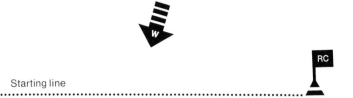

Starting line

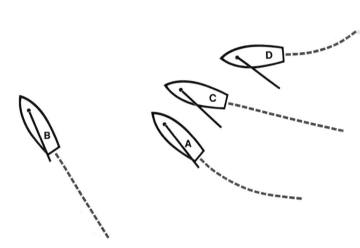

80-Q. In this race, two boats are moving ahead of you (Boat A) on your windward side as you approach the starting line. Your best maneuver is:

☐ Ease sheets and fall off.
☐ Trim sheets and luff up.

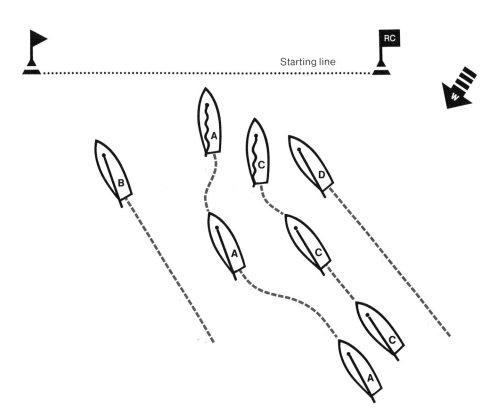

80-A.   Ease sheets and fall off. You have room below you, so use it to increase your forward speed by falling off and footing faster.

   When you have pulled ahead of the windward boats, then you trim sheets and luff them up. This puts you on their lee bow, where you can backwind them effectively.

   Strategy: Always keep your bow ahead of those of the boats to windward.

Starting line

81-Q. You (Boat A) are a little early for your start, but are luffing toward the line in excellent position.

Boat D is to windward and also luffing. Boats B and C are sailing faster courses astern and are overtaking you to leeward.

☐ Boats B and C are no threat.

☐ You should cross their bows now while you have the chance.

☐ You prefer to have Boats B and C on your leeward side anyway.

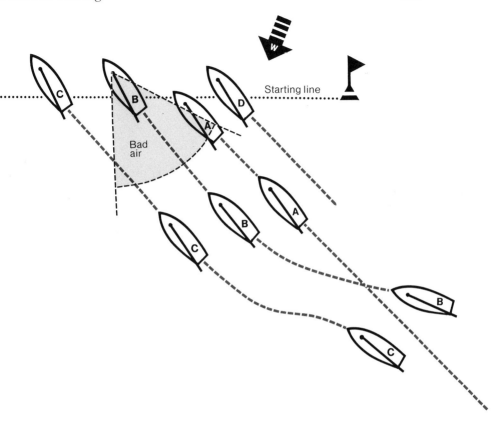

81-A. You should cross their bows now while you have the chance. Trim your sail and get moving. Only in this way can you stay on their lee bow and keep them under control.

Here (Fig. 81-A) you have neglected to watch B and C and they have gained a Safe Leeward Position. Now they are backwinding you and will move ahead rapidly.

Strategy: Prevent an overtaking boat from getting on your lee bow, even if it means moving down the line to another starting position.

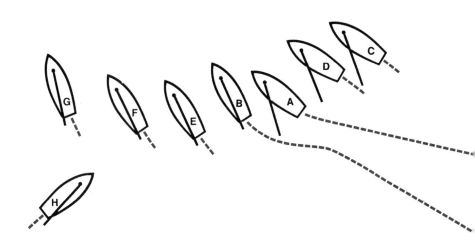

Starting line

82-Q. You (Boat A) have approached the line on a close reach, but Boat B is on your lee bow. There are no openings in the line of starting boats.

☐ You have had it.
☐ You should drop behind Boat D and tack.
☐ You should make yourself an opening.

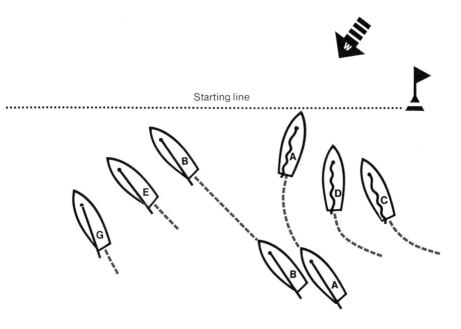

Starting line

82-A. You should make yourself an opening. By luffing the boats to windward, you can clear space on your leeward side and keep out of the backwind of Boat B and the other leeward boats.

Strategy: When you approach the starting line, keep pushing the windward boats up, to give yourself room below.

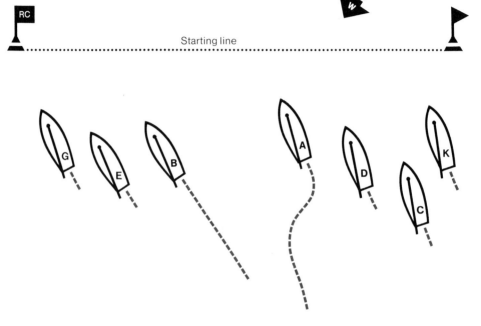

83-Q. You (Boat A) have worked hard to luff up the windward
boats and avoid the leeward boats. Now that you have a
hole in the line, how will you use it?
  With 10 seconds to go before the start, you should:

☐ Ease sheets and bear off slightly.
☐ Keep the hole open for emergencies.
☐ Trim sheets and harden up.

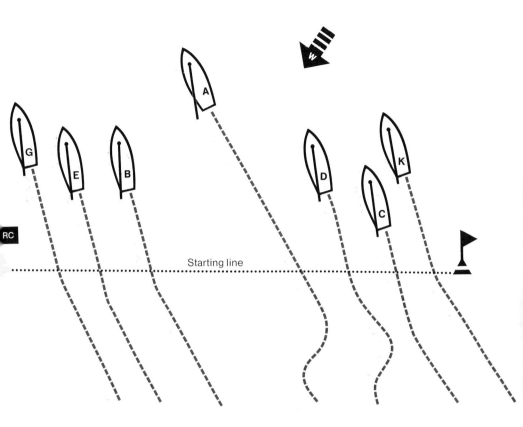

83-A. Ease sheets and bear off slightly. This allows you to foot faster than the other starters, most of whom harden up in the last 10 seconds and lose headway while trying to work up to windward. By footing faster rather than pinching, you are able to pull ahead into clear wind and will have a substantial lead before you must harden up.

Strategy: Use your room at the line to move out fast, and do not pinch.

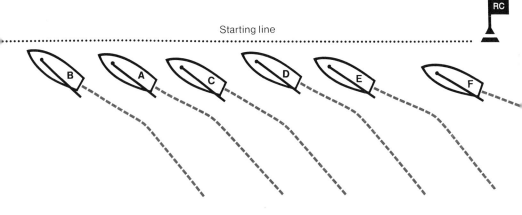

84-Q. Sudden wind shift one minute before the start! You (Boat A) are now backwinded by Boat B and cannot tack because of Boats C and D. You want to tack into this header. Can you?

☐ No; stay put and take your medicine.
☐ Yes; fall off and jibe onto port tack.
☐ Yes; pinch up and try to get clear of Boats C and
   D.

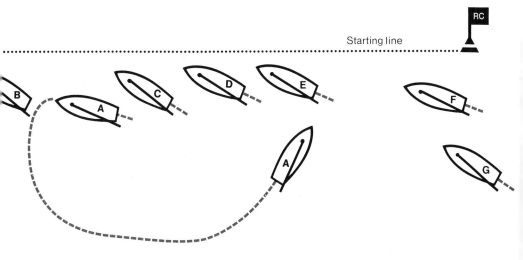

84-A. Yes; fall off and jibe onto port tack. You can then work back along the line and try to find a hole behind one of the starboard-tack boats and sail through on port into the favoring shift.

There will not be many holes in this line of starboard-tack boats, so do not try this in a large fleet or if many other boats are jibing over to port. In those circumstances, it may be to your advantage to sail into the header farther, while waiting for Boats C and D to tack.

Strategy: When sudden wind shifts put you in a poor position, take more chances, but get your wind clear.

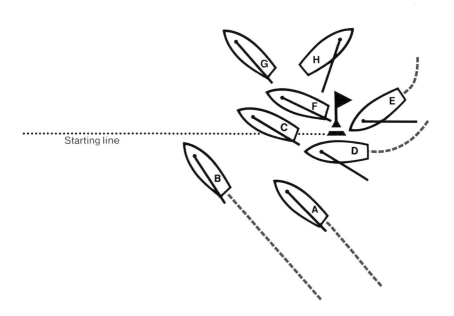

85-Q.   This race was started in a very light wind. You (Boat A)
and Boat B have found enough wind to make the starting
line, but when you arrive, it is cluttered with drifting
boats almost directly in your path.

Your best course is:

☐   To luff up Boat D, which is barging.
☐   Between Boats B and C.
☐   Below Boat B.

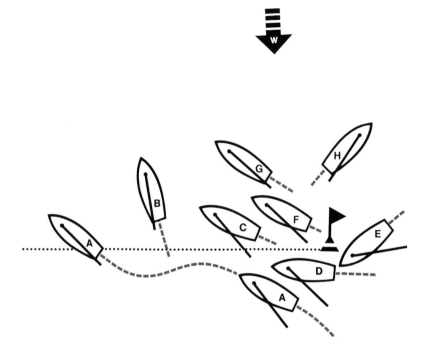

85-A. Below Boat B. In a drifting match, a cluster of boats like this one is poison; the disturbed air around them will trap any boat that gets too near. Falling off below B gives you increased boat speed, which will help you move away and into clearer air.

Strategy: In light wind, avoid groups of boats, keep moving, and do not pinch.

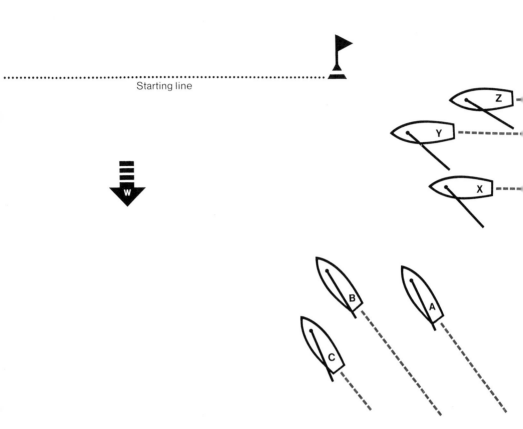

Starting line

86-Q. There are dangers in trying for the perfect start at the windward end. In your fleet you probably know how most of the other boats start. Boats B and C will try for the middle of the line. Boats X, Y, and Z consistently barge. You (Boat A) are trying for the windward-end position.

☐ This is a poor tactic.
☐ Boats X, Y, and Z cannot interfere with your start.
☐ Boat B is more dangerous than Boats X, Y, and Z.

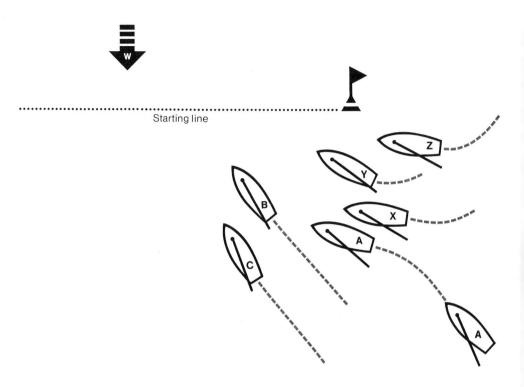

Starting line

86-A. This is a poor tactic.

You have right of way over the barging boats, and you may have one or all of them disqualified. However, they have ruined your start by cutting your wind and making you fall off, so you will not have gained a thing.

Strategy: Unless you are an expert, avoid the bargers at the windward end and get clear wind farther down the line.

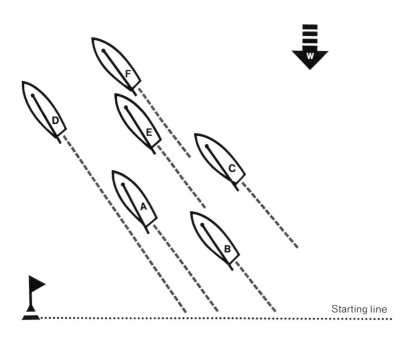

Starting line

87-Q. You are Boat A.

☐ Your position is hopeless.
☐ You should fall off.
☐ You should drop behind Boat B.

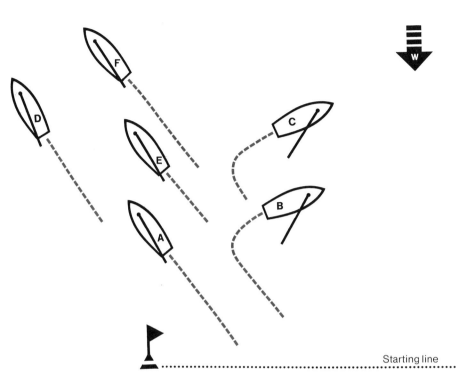

87-A. Your position is hopeless. You are being severely back-winded by Boats D, E, and F, and cannot tack because of the boat behind and to windward.

Your only hope is that Boat B or Boat C will tack. They are backwinded also and will want to clear their wind, so this is your best bet. If you fall off below Boat D, you will lose much distance before you get clear air.

Strategy: Take your medicine, and do not get into this position again. When you do tack, try not to do so in other boats' backwind.

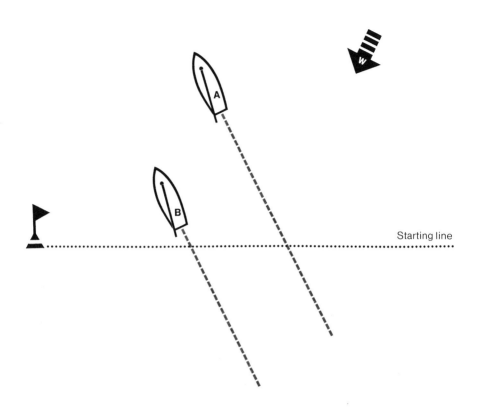

Starting line

88-Q.   You (Boat A) are trimmed in tight after the start and are beating to windward.

Boat B is below you and seems to be moving faster. Is there any way to stop her?

☐   No; any defense is illegal.
☐   Yes; stop pinching and ease your sheets.
☐   Tack at once.

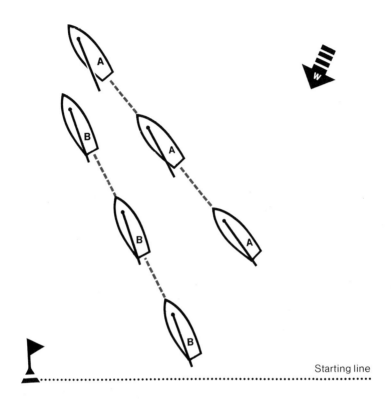

Starting line

88-A.   Yes; stop pinching and ease your sheets.

   It is illegal to fall off to prevent a boat from passing to leeward. However, it is legal to foot faster (that is, not point so high to gain hull speed) and blanket her, as long as you remain close-hauled.

   Strategy: Defend against a faster boat to leeward by footing rather than pointing, and work your way directly in front of her.

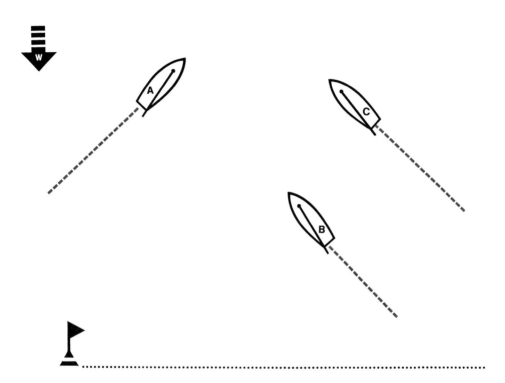

89-Q. The wind has been shifting all day — varying from north, where it is now, to northeast, where it is expected soon.

Because of this, you decide to work over to the star-board side of the course. However, on the way you are confronted with a crossing situation with Boats B and C on starboard tack. You can cross B safely, but not Boat C. You should:

☐ Fall off behind them both, despite the loss of five or six boat lengths.

☐ Tack between them, backwinding one and blanketing the other.

☐ Tack in front of Boat B.

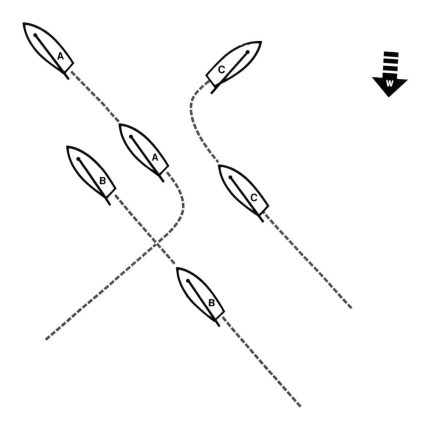

89-A. You goofed. You tacked between them to backwind B and blanket C. However, Boat C tacked immediately and is now headed for the favored side of the course, while you are headed away from it.

You should have fallen off behind them both, despite the loss of five or six boat lengths. Being on the side of the course that the expected wind shift will favor is more important than saving a few boat lengths. Besides, you should have known Boat C would tack.

Strategy: Do not force another boat to tack if it will put her in a more favorable position.

Expected
wind shift

Present
wind

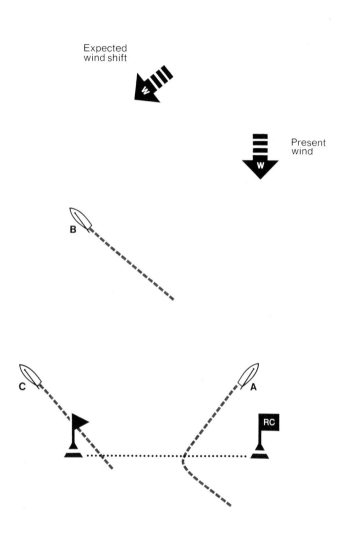

90-Q. Boat B has a commanding lead. If the wind shifts as expected:

☐ Boat A will take the lead.
☐ Boat B will retain the lead.
☐ Boat C will gain.

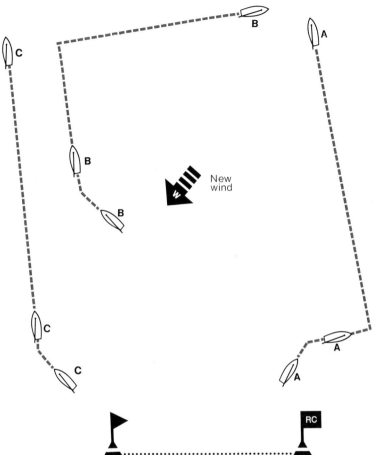

New
wind

90-A. Boat A will take the lead.

. In the first race, Boat A saw that the wind was shifting between north and northeast. Consequently, she kept to the northeast (starboard) side of the course in anticipation of the next shift in wind.

When it came, the shift put Boat A *as far up to windward* as Boat B. When they tack, Boat A is on starboard tack and is the first boat around the windward mark.

Strategy: Sail on the side of the course from which the expected wind shift will come. Know the local wind pattern everywhere you sail.

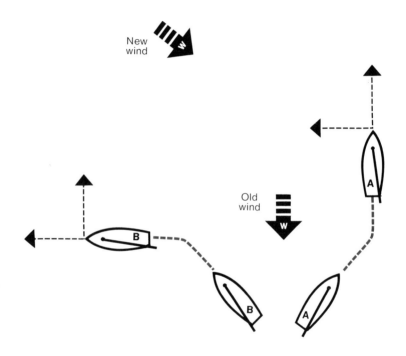

91-Q. On the beat up to the next mark, Boats A and B are in a wind shift, but on opposite tacks.

       ☐ Boat A should tack.
       ☐ Boat B should tack.
       ☐ Neither should tack.
       ☐ Both should tack.

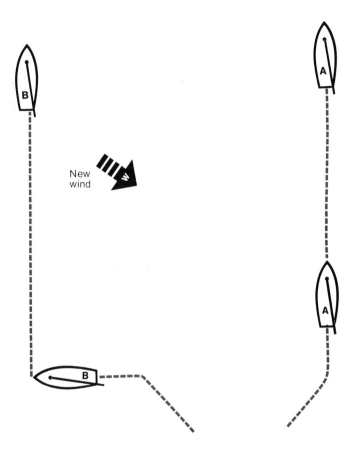

91-A. Boat B should tack. The proper course for each boat is the one that goes nearest the next mark. B is headed by the new wind and A is lifted, so B has to tack in order to sail a course that takes advantage of the shift.

How can you tell which tack offers the advantage?

Strategy: In variable winds, take the course that heads nearest the mark.

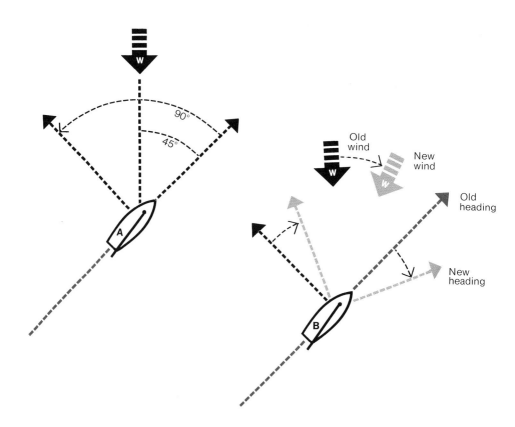

92. Boat A shows that a close-hauled boat sails at about a 45-degree angle to the direction of the wind. This means the opposite tack is 90 degrees away from the boat's present direction.

When the wind shifts, this right angle also shifts, as shown by Boat B, which is headed.

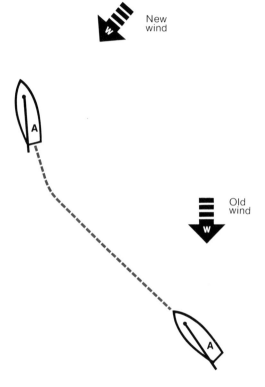

93-Q. You are sailing for the windward mark when the wind changes direction.

☐ You should tack at once.
☐ You should not tack.
☐ There is no way to tell whether it is best to tack or not.

93-A. You should not tack. The new wind has lifted you closer to the windward mark. Tacking would take you away from the mark.

Windward
mark

New
wind

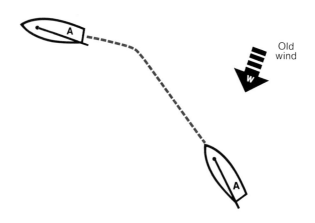

Old
wind

94-Q. Again while approaching the windward mark, you find the wind has shifted.

☐ You should tack at once.
☐ You should not tack.
☐ No way to tell.

94-A. You should tack at once. The wind has headed you, and you are sailing away from the windward mark. The opposite tack will lead you almost directly to the mark.

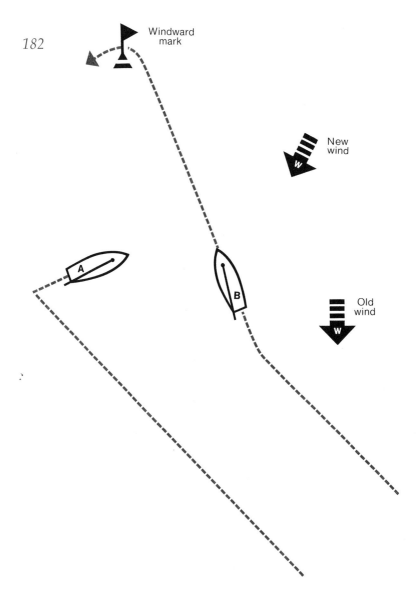

Windward mark

New wind

Old wind

95-Q. You and Boat B were having quite a race to the windward mark, with you in the lead. Just when you tacked to cross B's bow, the wind shifted. You were headed off and Boat B was lifted. If you hold your course, you will pass astern of B.

☐ You should tack at once.
☐ You should hold course to the lay line (Boat B's course).

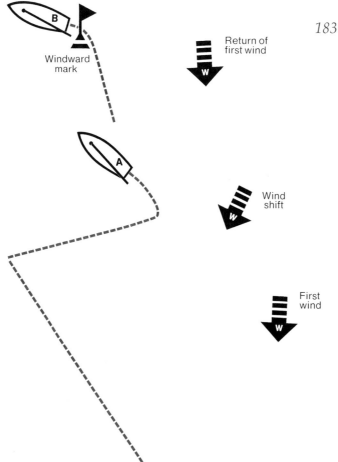

Return of
first wind

Windward
mark

Wind
shift

First
wind

95-A. You should hold course to the lay line (Boat B's course). Here you did the right thing, but at the wrong time. When you tacked on the lay line, the wind shifted back to its first direction and you unfortunately were headed once more.

The problem is that you are tacking out of phase with the wind shifts, and losing twice as much as the other boats gain. This close to the windward mark, there is not much else you can do now.

The mistake was in your first tack. You should have waited to see which way the wind was shifting before tacking, and then gotten into phase.

Strategy: When you tack in shifting winds, be sure you are in phase.

Windward
mark

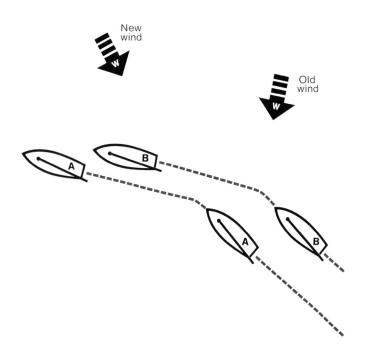

New
wind

Old
wind

96-Q. You are in a great race with Boat B for the windward mark
when a wind shift heads you off.

B is too close on your quarter to permit you to tack. What
do you do now?

☐ Fall off and tack behind Boat B.
☐ Hold course and wait for Boat B to tack.
☐ Pinch hard, dump more bad air on B, try to tack
later.

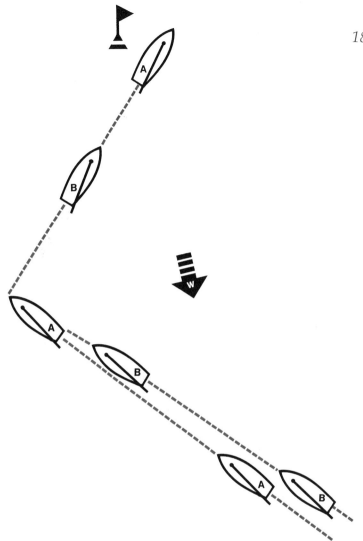

96-A. Pinch hard, dump more bad air on B, try to tack later. This is your best tactic, but it means you must get far enough ahead of B to tack safely.

Falling off will give the race to Boat B.

Your hope is that B will not be able to stay on your quarter, preventing you from tacking. If B tacks you should tack with her at once, so that you can prevent her from flopping onto starboard tack near the mark.

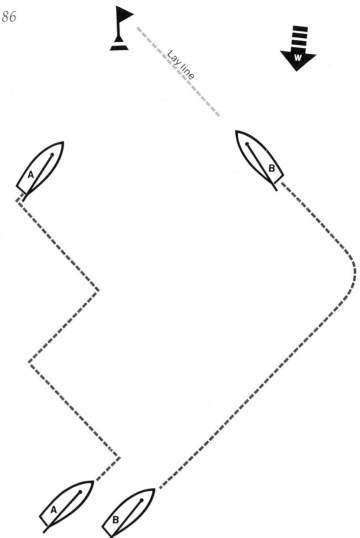

97-Q. If you were sailing alone, how would you approach the windward mark?

Boat A goes upwind in a series of tacks, while Boat B takes one long tack to the lay line.

☐ Boat A's course is better.
☐ Boat B's course is better.

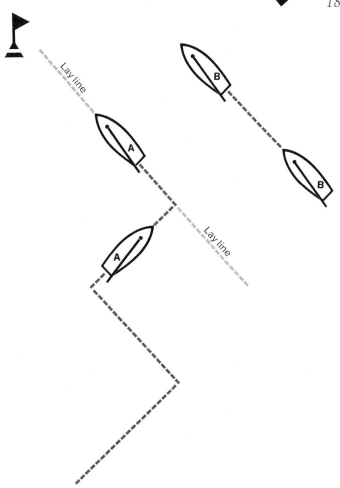

97-A. Boat A's course is better. Boat B is so far away from the mark when she tacks her one long tack that she has a good chance of missing it, particularly of overstanding (sailing beyond the mark), as shown here.

By taking shorter tacks, Boat A sails closer to the mark and is able to judge the lay line more accurately. If any wind shift lifts her, Boat A can take advantage of it; B cannot, because she is already on the lay line.

Boat A more than makes up for the loss of boat lengths inherent in frequent tacking by being able to take advantage of wind shifts and having more accuracy in laying the mark.

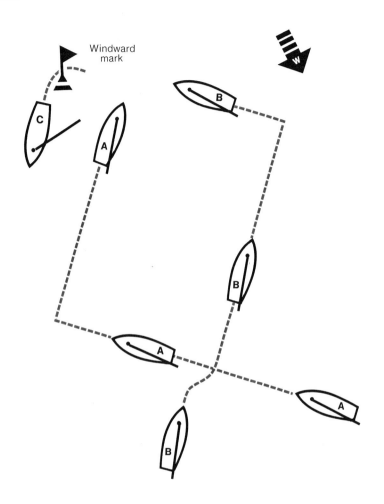

Windward mark

W

98-Q. Boat B fell off for extra speed and safely crossed your bow. When you tacked for the mark, you found she was bearing down on you on starboard tack.

☐ You should tack at once and claim buoy room.
☐ You should have tacked before Boat B could cross your bow.
☐ You should have tacked just after Boat B crossed your bow.

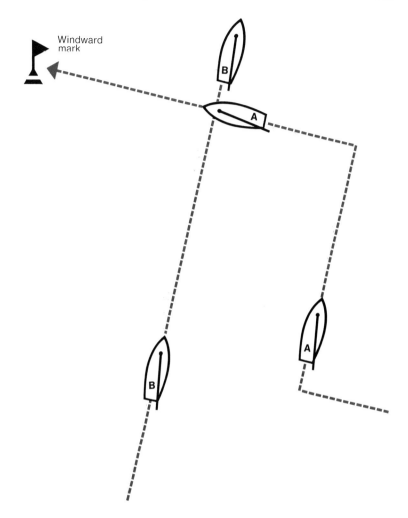

98-A. You should have tacked before Boat B could cross your bow.

You want to approach the mark on starboard, with right of way over B, without having to tack near the mark. Consequently, you must sail for the lay line, come about onto starboard, and complete your tack before reaching Boat B's course.

This will reverse the crossing situation, giving you right of way. B may not tack in front of you.

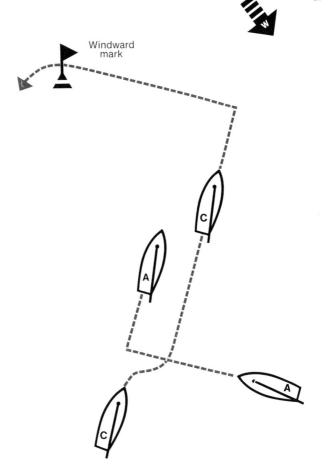

Windward mark

99-Q. In a similar situation, approaching the mark, Boat C crossed your bow on port tack, so you tacked at once. You are now in a:

☐ Poor position; you have tacked into Boat C's backwind and cannot beat her to the mark.

☐ Good position; you can prevent Boat C from tacking for the mark before you.

☐ Risky position; either of these may happen and you cannot control which.

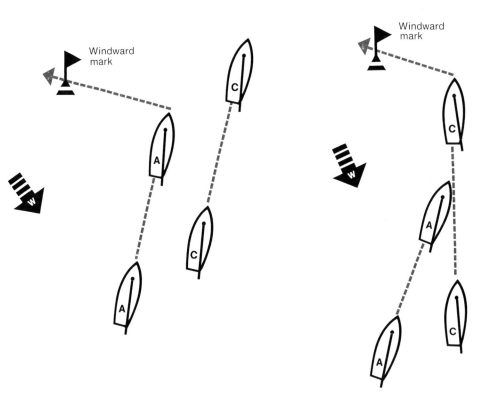

99-A. You are now in a risky position. If Boat C is able to pinch up enough to keep you from clearing her backwind, she will be first at the mark (right diagram).

If she is unable to keep you in her backwind (left diagram), or if the distance to the mark is so short that backwinding is not effective, then you can prevent C from tacking by holding your course. She may not tack in front of you and must wait for you to head for the mark.

Thus, your position is precarious. This maneuver calls for too much finesse and luck.

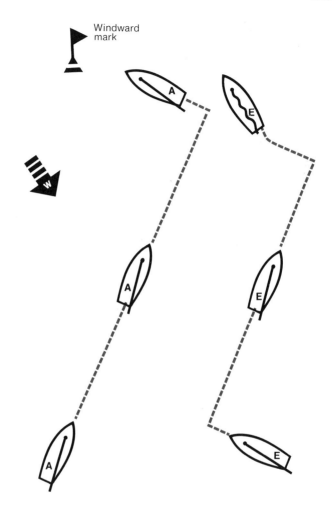

Windward
mark

100-Q. You tried to sneak in on the lay line ahead of Boat E, but
she had to luff up to avoid hitting you, and you are therefore disqualified.

What could you have done to avoid this and still be in
a good position?

☐   Tack short of Boat E's course.
☐   Fall off astern of Boat E, then tack for the mark.

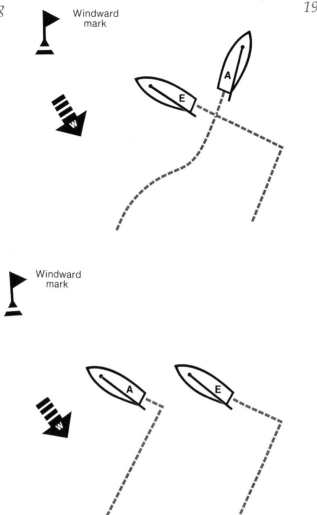

100-A. Fall off astern of Boat E, then tack for the mark (upper diagram). You would lose a few boat lengths, but you would still be in the race.

    If you tacked short of Boat E's course (lower diagram), you would probably not make the mark. You need to have a lot of way on before you dare shoot the mark from below the lay line.

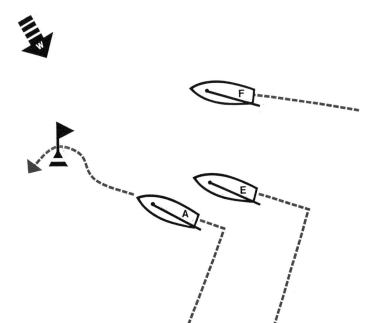

101-Q. Boat E claims "foul" if you (Boat A) shoot the mark. Is he right?

☐ Yes.
☐ No.

Why?

101-A. No. You are the leeward boat and have the right to luff Boat E (NAYRU Rule 38.1).

Shooting the mark is a good tactic, provided you have enough way on to carry you around. Otherwise there is trouble.

102-Q. You (Boat A) tried to shoot the mark but missed.

What must you do now?

☐ Take one penalty turn around the mark and then round it correctly.

☐ Jibe onto port tack and try again.

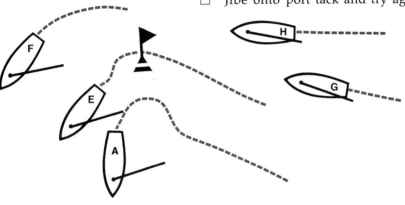

102-A. Jibe onto port tack and try again.

You did not hit the mark, so no penalty turn is required and you have all your rights. In approaching the mark on port tack, however, you have to give way to Boats G and H on starboard. Instead of being a contender for the lead, you are four boats behind.

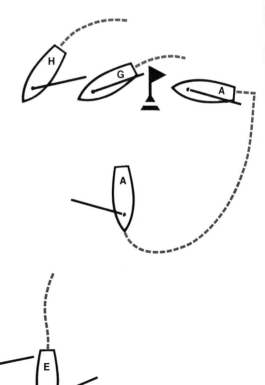

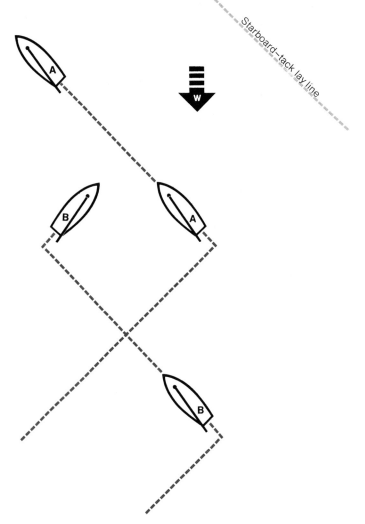

103-Q. Covering a competitor means staying upwind of her at all times. You tack when she tacks, and you give her your backwind or blanket cone whenever possible. If she is too far away to be affected by your bad air, you simply stay between her and the next mark.

Here you have been covering Boat B on the beat to windward. Boat B has just tacked from under your cover.

- ☐ You should tack at once, but go only as far as the lay line.
- ☐ You should keep on present course and sail to the port lay line.
- ☐ Boat B was in error and should not have tacked.

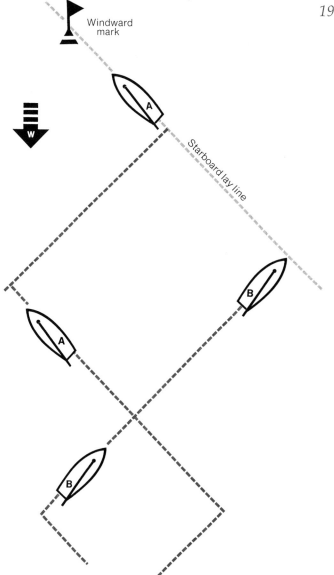

103-A. You should tack at once, but go only as far as the lay line. You have remained upwind of Boat B as long as possible. If you stay with her longer, you will be above the lay line and will overstand the mark.

Boat B was correct in tacking when she did, both to clear her air and to try to drive you above the lay line.

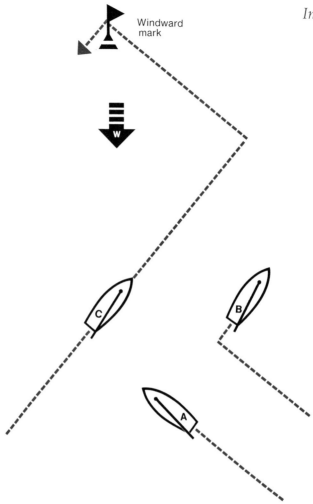

Windward
mark

104-Q. You got behind and Boat B covered you. Now Boat C is crossing your bow on port tack. You had hoped to approach the mark on starboard tack on the lay line. What do you do now?

☐ Tack quickly to leeward of Boat C and head for the lay line.

☐ Tack on Boat C's course and head for the lay line.

☐ Hold your course and approach the mark on port tack.

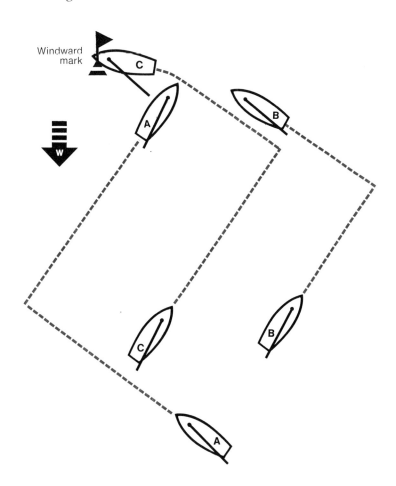

Windward mark

104-A. Hold your course and approach the mark on port tack.

In this way you will have free air and will avoid the backwind from Boats B and C.

You can hope for a lift to fetch the mark—or more realistically, for a hole in the line of starboard-tack boats on the lay line.

Windward
mark

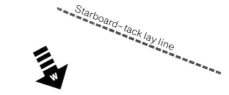

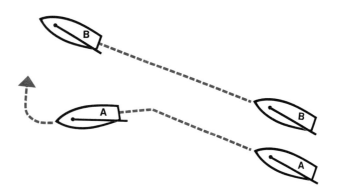

105-Q. Boat B has been covering you like a tent for most of the weather leg. You have a Safe Leeward Position, but B is so close she prevents you from tacking. You fall off to tack, intending to tack under her and head for the starboard lay line.

How can B prevent you from escaping cover?

☐   Tack when you tack.
☐   Sail to the port-tack lay line, then tack.

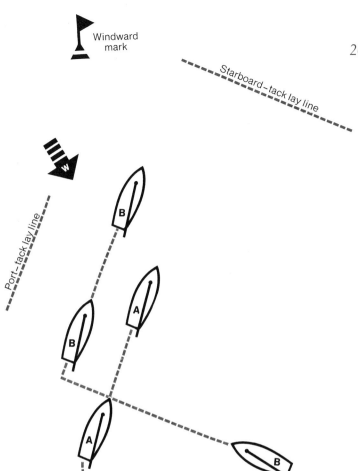

Windward mark

Starboard-tack lay line

Port-tack lay line

W

105-A. Tack when you tack. In this way, Boat B can keep between you and the mark and prevent you from tacking
at the lay line ahead of her. If B made any other maneuver, you could get far enough to leeward of her to
have room to tack on the starboard lay line and approach
the mark on starboard tack.

Windward
mark

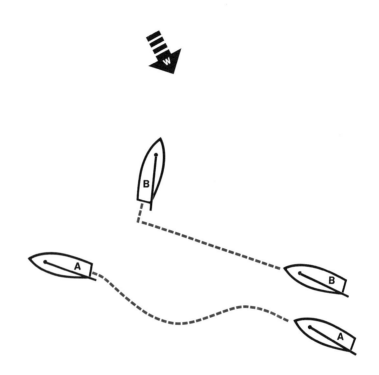

106-Q. Here Boat B saw you fall off to tack and tacked quickly
to cover. She did it too soon, however—giving you an
opportunity to change your plans. Your defense was not
to tack at all.

Now Boat B will approach the mark on the starboard-
tack lay line, which is in her favor.

Can you take away her advantage?

☐ No.
☐ Yes; tack close to Boat B on her windward
quarter.
☐ Yes; sail to the port-tack lay line before coming
about, thus saving yourself the distance of
B's extra tack.

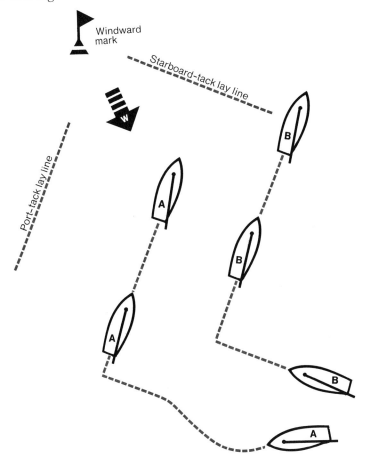

Windward mark

Starboard-tack lay line

Port-tack lay line

106-A. Yes; tack close to Boat B on her windward quarter. This will prevent Boat B from tacking for the mark because of the "Tacking Too Close" Rule (NAYRU Rule 41.1).

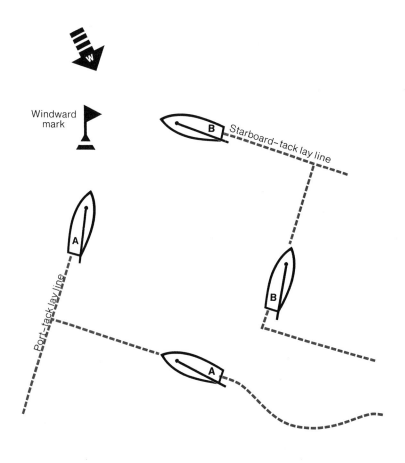

107. Had you chosen not to tack (as in 106-A) and sailed instead to the port-tack lay line, you would have found Boat B had the right of way as starboard *boat* at the mark. This would be to your disadvantage.

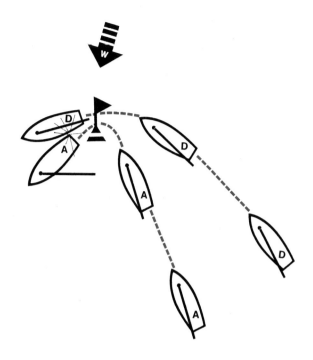

108-Q. As you are rounding the windward mark, your stern swings wide and hits Boat D.

    ☐ You should disqualify yourself.
    ☐ You should go around the mark again.
    ☐ Boat D is at fault, and you should continue the race.

108-A. Boat D is at fault, and you should continue the race.
    Two rules apply here. Boat D is the windward boat and must keep clear of you. Secondly, under the "Buoy Room" Rule, Boat D must allow room for you to round the mark and must anticipate that your stern may swing wide. Boat D is disqualified.

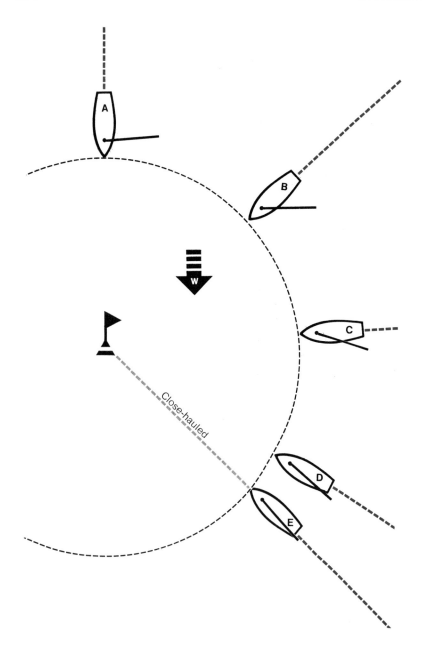

109. Which boat will get to the mark first?

Once you round the windward mark, you begin the downhill portion of the race, sailing one or two lazy legs offwind before another hard beat.

Nevertheless, good planning for these legs will let you pick up any number of boats that sail too casually. You want to know which is the favored side of the course, which tack will give you the most advantage, and what is the fastest course to the leeward mark.

One important aspect of your strategy is knowing that a boat's speed is governed by her point of sailing. As a boat sails closer to the wind she goes faster, up to a few degrees below close-hauled.

Here all boats are the same distance from the mark. Which boat will get there first?

Boat D will. Hers is the fastest point of sailing.

Boat C will beat B, and Boat B will beat A. This means the boats on a reach will travel faster than the boats on a run.

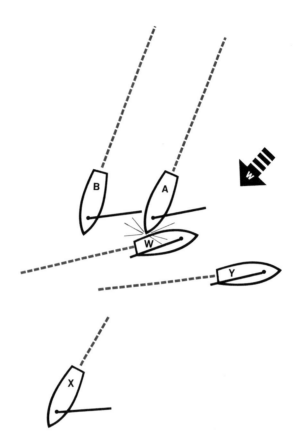

110-Q. Collision! You did not see Boat W because Boat B was blocking your line of vision. Now you have hit her amidships.

    ☐ You are disqualified and must drop out of the race.

    ☐ You are not disqualified.

110-A. You are not disqualified.

    You are the windward boat and must keep clear of leeward boats on the same tack. But Boat W is on port tack and you are on starboard, so here the Opposite Tack Rule applies and you have right of way. If you had jibed onto port tack for your leeward leg, you would have been at a serious disadvantage.

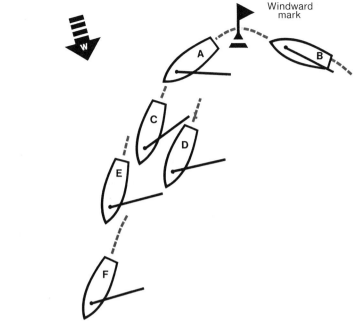

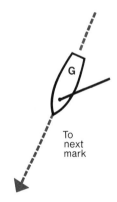

111-Q. You have just rounded the windward mark in the middle of the fleet. Now you will have to sail through the choppy water and turbulent air caused by the other boats. All of this will slow you down.

Which is the best course?

☐ Follow the straight line to the next mark.
☐ Sail above the fleet now and come down on them later.
☐ Sail below the fleet now and come up to them later.

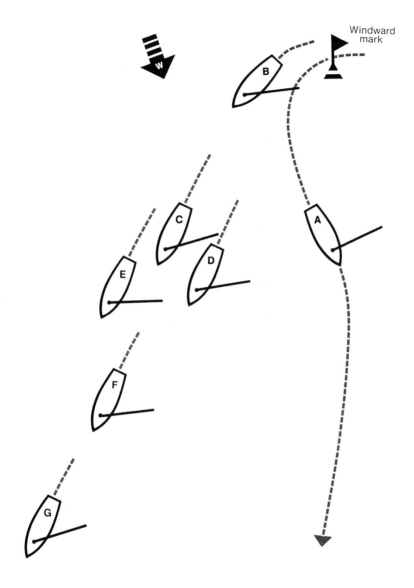

111-A. Sail below the fleet now and come up to them later.

By doing this you not only get away from the turbulent air and choppy wake of the other boats, but also avoid being blanketed.

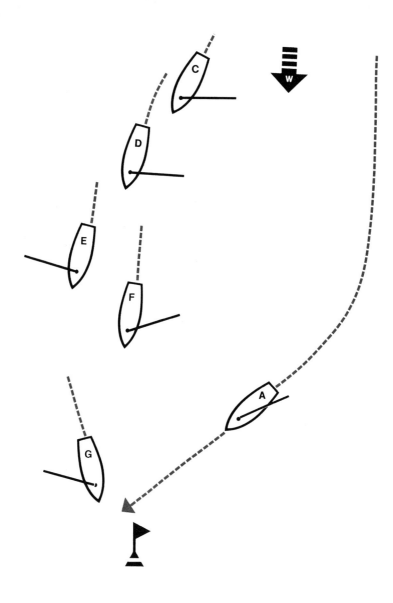

112-Q. The longer distance you sail by taking your course well below the fleet is offset by your clear air and undisturbed water and arriving on a faster point of sailing at the leeward mark.

    ☐ True.
    ☐ False.

112-A. True. Your freedom from involvement with other boats will allow you to keep your position while you fall off on the slower point of sailing (the run being slower than the reach). Now, approaching the mark, you are on the faster course, a reach, while the fleet bears down on a run. You will probably be leeward boat and have right of way as well as good boat speed for maneuvering at the mark.

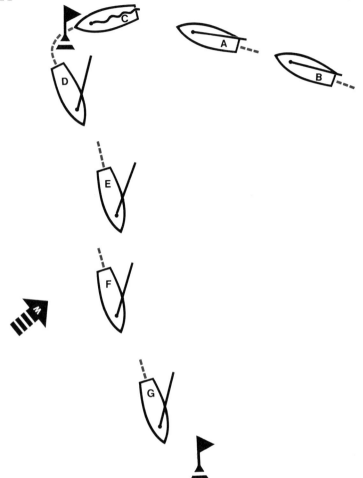

113-Q.   This is a close reach. As you round the windward mark,
you have to choose which course to sail on.

☐   Sail the straight-line course to the next mark.
☐   Sail high at first, then drop down on the mark.
☐   Drop below the fleet, then sail up to the mark.

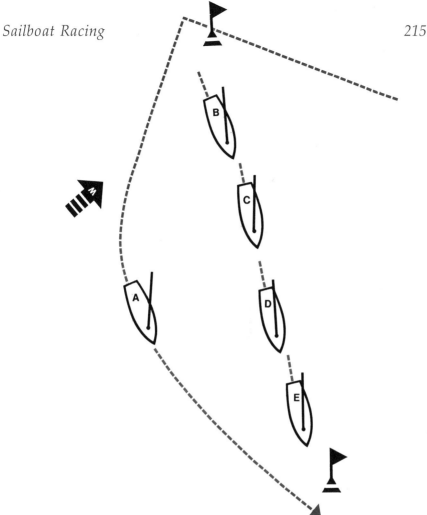

113-A. Sail high at first, then drop down on the mark.

As a general rule, the slow portion of a reach should be sailed first—which means most reaches are best sailed to leeward. A close reach, however, is better sailed to windward, because if the wind shifts a few degrees, the reach will become a beat.

Any boat caught to leeward will have to take some extra tacks to fetch the mark. By sailing close-hauled at the start of the leg, you protect yourself against this eventuality. If the boats on the line have to sail close-hauled to the mark, you will be above them on the faster point of sailing.

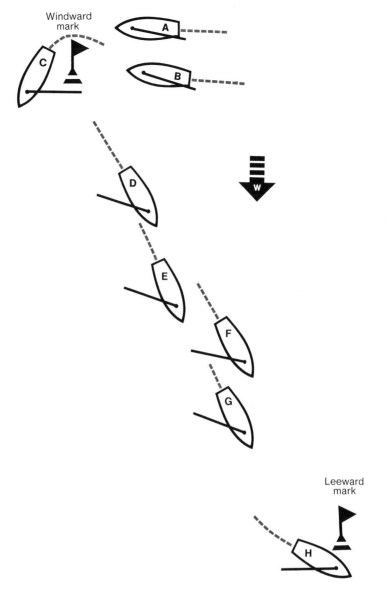

114-Q. You may wish to sail your reach differently according to whether the wind is freshening or dropping.

As you round the windward mark, you find the wind starting to drop. What is your course?

☐ Fall off on a run, then harden up near the mark.
☐ Sail a close reach upwind of the fleet, then fall off near the mark.

Boat B rounds the mark and finds that the wind is freshening. What is her course?

☐ Sail high initially, then drop down.
☐ Drop down first, then sail a close reach.

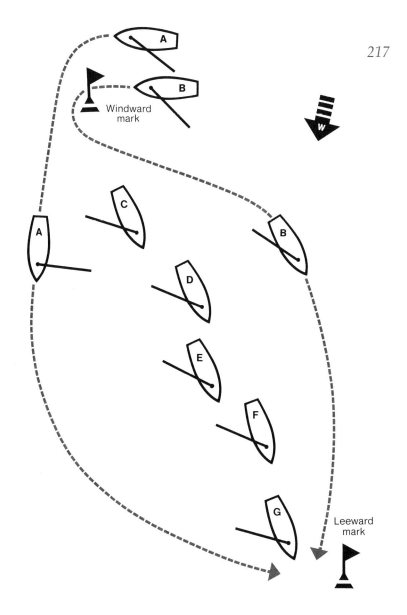

114-A.   You (Boat A) should fall off on a run, then harden up near the mark.

Boat B should sail high initially, then drop down.

In both cases the boats will sail the slow part of the leg in the strong wind, saving the faster point of sailing for the lesser wind and thus getting the jump on the competition.

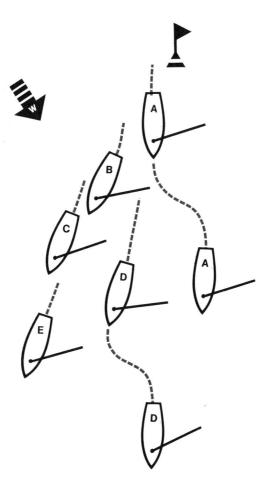

115-Q. You (Boat A) round the windward mark and turn sharply to leeward behind a close group of boats. Suddenly Boat D, who was ahead and to windward, drops down in front of you.

What should you do now?

    ☐ Fall off and try to pass her to leeward.
    ☐ Head up and try to pass her to windward.
    ☐ Yell and protest.

115-A. Yell and protest. Boat D is committing a foul (NAYRU Rule 39). You are within three boat lengths of D, so she may not fall off to prevent you from passing to leeward.

You do not have enough clear air to work back up to windward, and if you fall off, Boat D will probably drop down in front of you again. Your hope is that you can make Boat D move out of your way.

116-Q. On this run, you (Boat A) are in a good position on the leeward side of the fleet. The wind is brisk. You find that if you head up and sail almost 60 degrees to your present course, you can plane. However, planing will take you to the other side of the fleet, where you will not be in a position to claim room at the mark.

You should:

☐ Get on the plane.
☐ Hold your course and play your position.

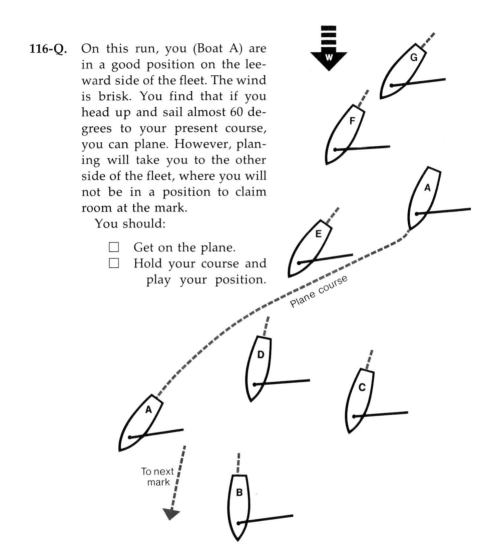

116-A. Get on the plane.

Planing increases the speed above the boat's normal maximum, and the extra distance gained this way more than offsets the distance you go off course or out of position.

Strategy: When you have a chance to do it, always plane.

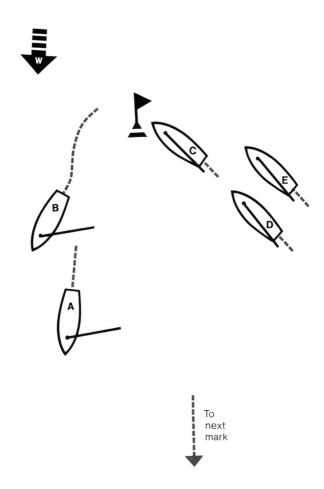

117-Q. You have rounded the windward mark in the lead and are now on the downwind leg. Boat B threatens to pass you to windward. What should you do?

☐ Fall off to leeward.
☐ Harden up to windward.
☐ Stay on a middle course.

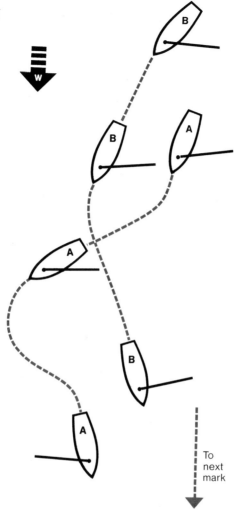

To
next
mark

117-A. Harden up to windward — but do not get into a luffing match.

There are times when any of the above alternatives would be appropriate. If Boat B has enough speed to pass you to windward, there is little you can do anyway. However, you do not want to be drawn out of position so that the overtaking boat can pass to leeward, which Boat B is doing here.

A luffing match would only remove you from the race. That is what has happened to Boats C and D.

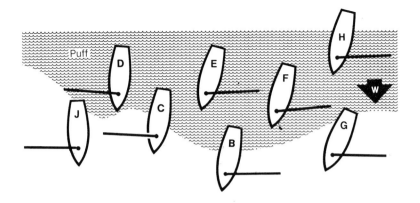

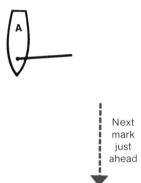

Next
mark
just
ahead

118-Q. The weekly calamity. You are well ahead on the down-wind leg when the wind drops. Now the boats behind have a fresh puff and are bearing down on you with a massive blanket zone.

　　You are still moving, so what is your best course?

- ☐ Head up a little.
- ☐ Head up sharply.
- ☐ Fall off a little.
- ☐ Fall off sharply.
- ☐ Hold your course to the mark.

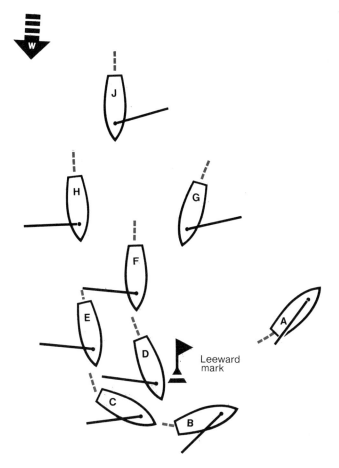

Leeward
mark

118-A. Hold your course to the mark. You are close enough to
the mark to sit tight and hope the wind will reach you
before the other boats do.

To have an advantage over the other boats on the next
leg, it is essential that you round the leeward mark first
or on the inside position. Therefore, moving far off
course, especially to windward, is not advisable here.

If you were a long way from the mark, your best bet
would be to see which side the new wind was coming
from and try to get there before the other boats reached
you.

Any of these answers is potentially correct, depending
on how far away the other boats are and how spread out
they are.

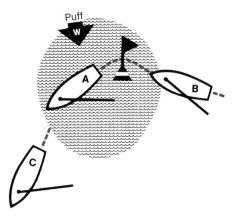

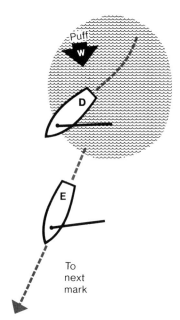

119-Q. You're in bad shape at the windward mark. Airs are light and puffy. You slide around easily in your own private breeze, then are faced with a choice. You should:

☐ Sail a little upwind to be the first to catch another puff.

☐ Blanket Boat C.

☐ Stay with the puff as long as you're going in the general direction of the next mark.

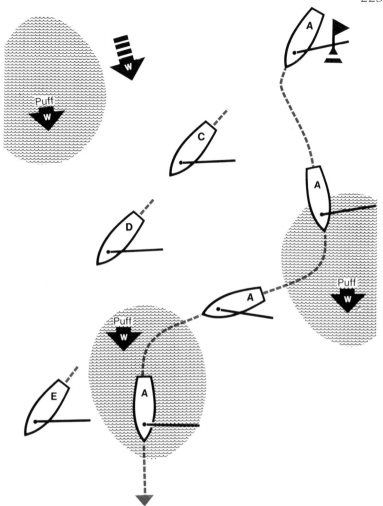

119-A. Stay with the puff as long as you're going in the general direction of the next mark. But continue to look for another puff, and dare an erratic course as long as you are moving with greater speed than the other boats.

Strategy: In light airs, be alert for new wind. Use puffs. Watch the water, other boats, and any other signs for new wind.

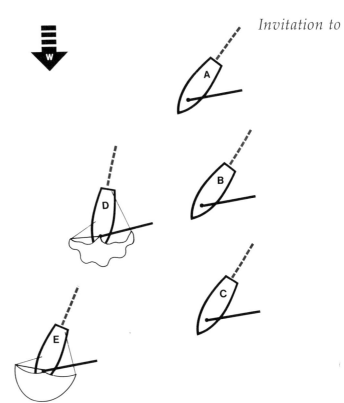

To
next
mark

120-Q. The lead boat has set her spinnaker successfully, and the
boat ahead of you is trying to set hers.
  You should:

☐ Set yours as fast as possible.
☐ Head up to blanket the boat ahead.
☐ Fall off to set your spinnaker.

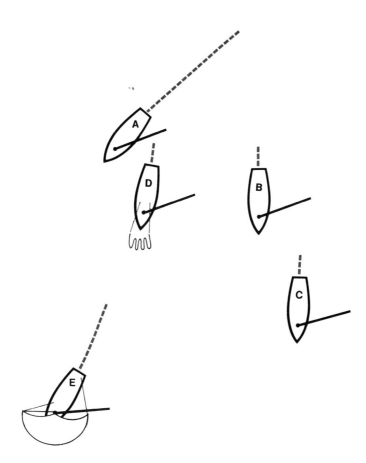

120-A. Head up to blanket the boat ahead. You can sail faster on the reach and can attack Boat D while she is vulnerable.

Strategy: Attack the other boat when she is setting spinnaker or bringing it in.

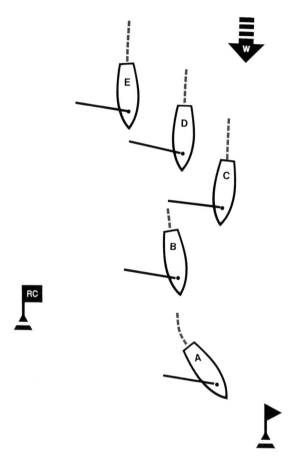

121-Q. This is the last time around the leeward mark, and you are in the lead. The most important thing now for you is to:

☐ Notice where the Race Committee is setting the finish line.

☐ Not jibe too soon.

☐ Cut close to the mark as you round it.

121-A. Notice where the Race Committee is setting the finish line. You can start to plot your course for the final leg as soon as you see the lay of the line and can determine if there is a favored end.

PART IV

Problems Encountered in
Sailing Tides and Currents
Logic and Mathematics Involved
Racing Tactics Special to Sailing in
Tides and Currents
Reading the Tidal or River Chart

Sooner or later, the problem of coping with flowing water faces a large proportion of skippers. At yacht clubs on rivers or in tidal basins, this skill must be learned along with the rudiments of sailing. A lake skipper, however, may never need the knowledge until he has won a club series and earned the privilege of racing in the "nationals" for his class.

There are rudimentary principles for sailing in a current. These must be understood before racing tactics that make use of this moving water can be applied.

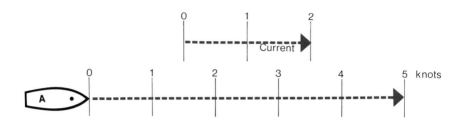

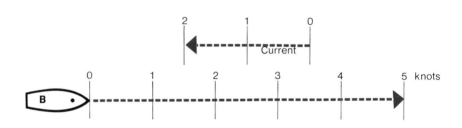

122-Q. How can you tell which way the tide or current will move you?

Boat A will go five (nautical) miles in one hour, but the current is flowing with her at two miles an hour. How far will A travel in that hour?

☐ Three miles.
☐ Five miles.
☐ Seven miles.

How about Boat B?

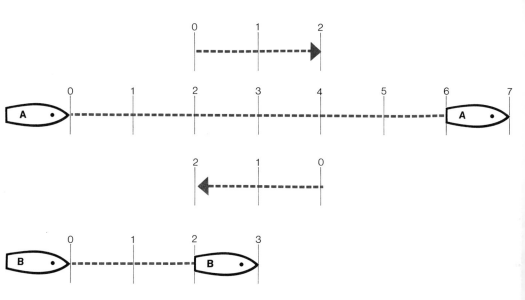

122-A. All problems of tide and current can be solved by elementary mathematics. Since the current is going in the same direction as Boat A, its effect is added to the speed of Boat A.

Boat A travels seven miles in one hour.

In Boat B's case, the current opposes her forward progress, so is subtracted.

Boat B travels three miles in one hour.

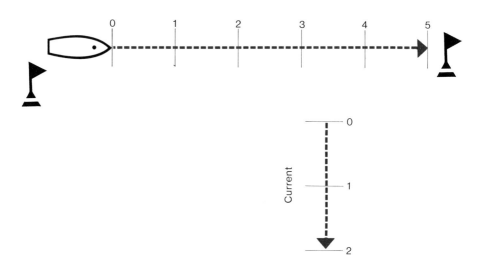

123-Q. Suppose the current is going across your course. How will you know where it will take you?

☐ Draw a vector diagram.
☐ You will have to guess.

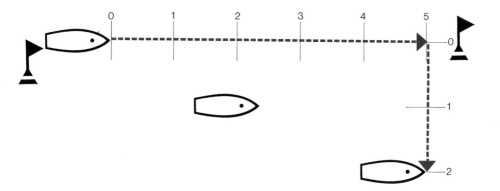

123-A. Draw a vector diagram. This means, draw an arrow whose direction is your course and whose length represents your boat speed. On the tip of this arrow, draw another in the direction of the current whose length represents the speed of the current. The tip of this second arrow will be your new position.

Here Boat A sails due east at five miles per hour and is moved off her course by a current running south at the rate of two miles per hour. If she travels for one hour without correction, she will be two miles from her destination.

Since the unit of speed is one knot, which is one nautical mile per hour, the diagram, for simplicity, is made for one hour. Once you know the effect of the current for this time, you can determine it for any part of an hour.

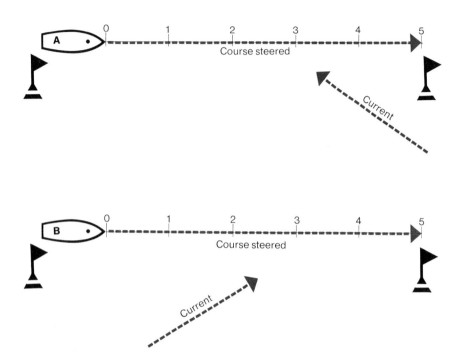

124-Q. How will Boat A and Boat B do in sailing this leg of their race, considering the current each has?

☐ Boat A will be moved beyond her mark.
☐ Both will be moved above their marks.
☐ Boat B will not reach her mark.

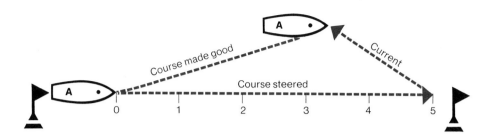

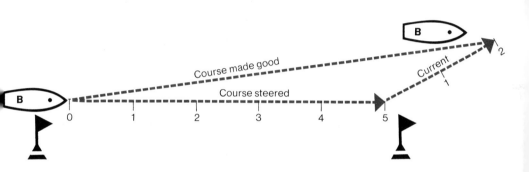

124-A. Both will be moved above their marks. The vector diagram of each boat's speed and current shows her new position. A line from the starting position to the new one shows the actual course made good.

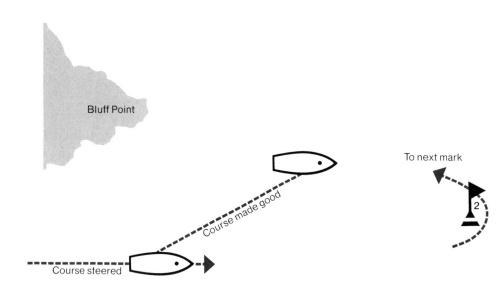

125-Q. In this race, the first time you tried to reach No. 2 Mark, you found yourself pushed north of the mark by the current around Bluff Point.

☐ You should steer south on an opposite course to the "course made good" the first time.

☐ You should tack due south to compensate for the current.

☐ The current is running south.

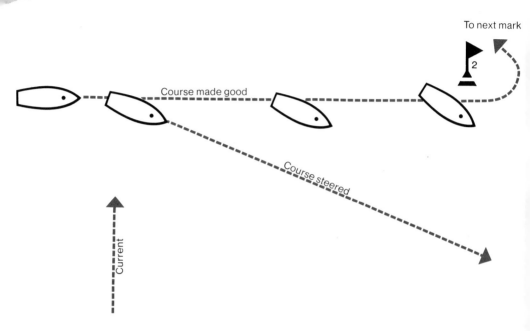

Bluff Point

To next mark

Course made good

Course steered

2

Current

125-A. You should steer south on an opposite course to the "course made good" the first time. The current is flowing north, so by your steering into the current, your "course made good" becomes the one to the mark.

Bellows
Point

Tide

To next mark

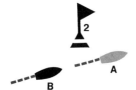

126-Q. Your regatta folder has indicated HT (high tide) at 1:20 P.M. The race begins at 10 A.M. Will this affect your course?

☐ It won't.

☐ You will expect fast water and will sail far into the tidal current.

☐ You can expect fast-moving water around 1 to 2 P.M.

126-A. You will expect fast water and will sail far into the tidal current. The water runs fastest during the time farthest from its low and high points, about six hours apart.

Here Boat B did not plot her course to compensate for the high speed of the current.

127-Q. How will the strategy change for a 1 P.M. start?

☐   It won't.

☐   A more direct course can be sailed to the mark.

☐   The flow stops about then.

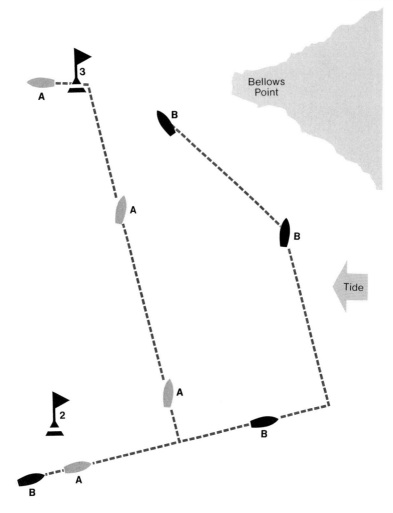

127-A. A more direct course can be sailed to the mark, since
around high tide or low tide the flow lessens, or almost
ceases, for a period of minutes to an hour, before it re-
verses direction and gains speed again.

    Well in advance of the race, question your hosts about
this for the regatta area, so that you can use the information in your pre-race warm-up.

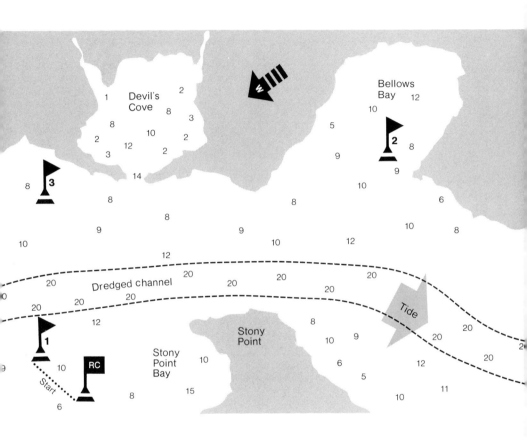

128-Q. This is the chart for a regatta in which you will compete. You should:

☐ Pay most attention to depth of water.
☐ Plastic-cover it to keep it dry on the boat.
☐ Study and test the tidal currents.

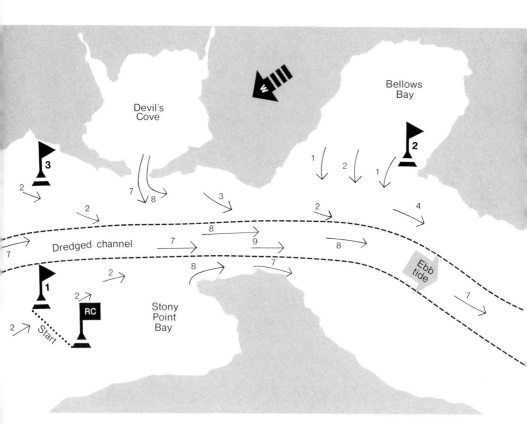

128-A. Study and test the tidal currents. By knowing where the currents run strongest, you can plan your strategy for every leg of the race—making maximum use of the favoring flow, and sailing against the current where it's weakest.

129-Q. Cut a boat shape out of stiff paper and use it to show the course you would take.

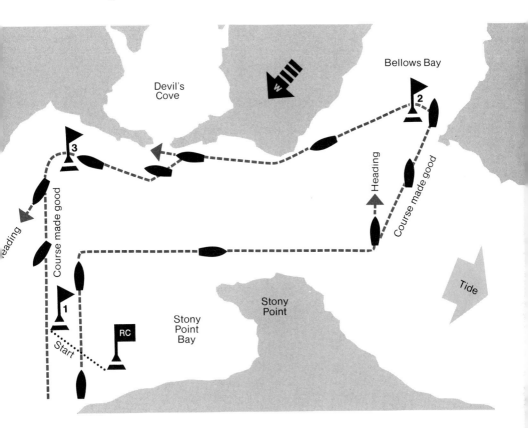

129-A. You sailed quickly for the dredged channel to take advantage of the swift current. Then came the tricky maneuver of crossing the current on a heading that would compensate (remember the vector diagrams!) for your expected sideslip. You assumed that during the ebbing tide the water would be running out of Devil's Cove, so you laid up of the mark. Again, crossing the current, you planned your course according to the speed of the flow.

Since this does require practice, get in some sailing time in tidal waters before racing there.

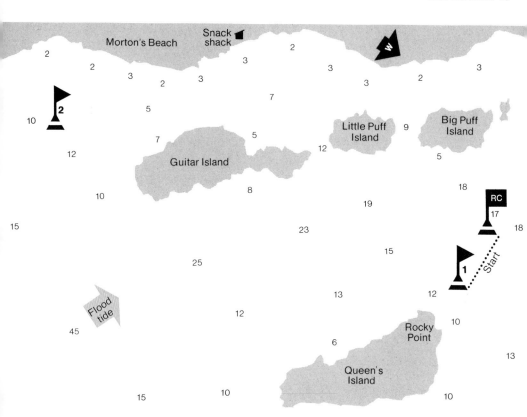

130-Q. There is no dredged channel at the Morton's Beach regatta. The tide will be high at 12:50 P.M., and the race starts at 9 A.M. Study the chart well to determine the location of favorable currents.

Most important to consider:

☐ The deepest readings.
☐ The wind direction.
☐ The overall flow pattern.

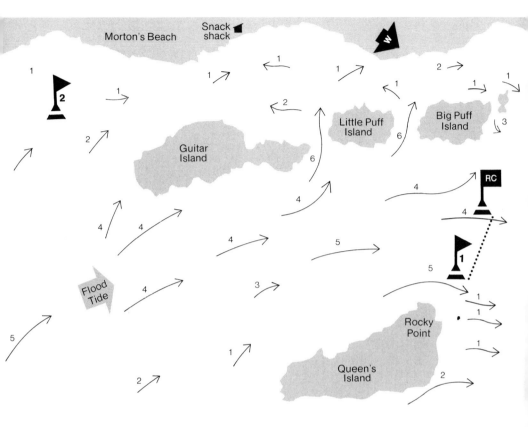

130-A. The overall flow pattern is most important to planning your course. Often water flows most swiftly through strictures, such as the narrows between islands. Best pre-race strategy is to discuss the course with a native from the host fleet.

131-Q. In this case the sailing plan with most to offer is:

☐ The wide channel where air is clearer.
☐ Between islands.

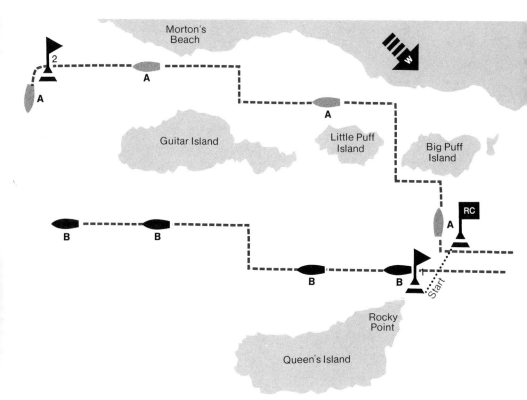

131-A. Between islands. You can thus take advantage of swift water, and will then be in favoring currents or slack water.

Skipper B, who chooses to sail the wide waters, has to buck faster current, which retards him even though he has fewer tacks to make.

APPENDIX
Official
Racing Rules

The following are portions of the racing rules of the North American Yacht Racing Union, adopted 1969, and are reprinted with permission. Complete copies of the official Racing Rules may be obtained from Corresponding Secretary, 37 West 44th Street, New York, New York 10036.

Listed below are excerpts from those sections of the rules of most interest to junior sailors and racing skippers.

PART I

DEFINITIONS

Racing — A yacht is **racing** from her preparatory signal until she has either **finished** and cleared the finishing line and finishing **marks** or retired, or until the race has been **cancelled, postponed** or **abandoned**, except that in match or team races, the sailing instructions may prescribe that a yacht is **racing** from any specified time before the preparatory signal.

Starting — A yacht **starts** when, after her starting signal, any part of her hull, crew or equipment first crosses the starting line in the direction of the first mark.

Finishing — A yacht **finishes** when any part of her hull, or of her crew or equipment in normal position, crosses the finishing line from the direction of the last mark.

Luffing — Altering course towards the wind until head to wind.

Tacking — A yacht is **tacking** from the moment she is beyond head to wind until she has **borne away**, if beating to windward, to a **close-hauled** course; if not beating to windward, to the course on which her mainsail has filled.

Bearing Away — Altering course away from the wind until a yacht begins to **jibe**.

Jibing — A yacht begins to **jibe** at the moment when, with the wind aft, the foot of her mainsail crosses her centre line and completes the **jibe** when the mainsail has filled on the other **tack**.

On a Tack — A yacht is **on a tack** except when she is **tacking** or **jibing**. A yacht is on the **tack** (**starboard** or **port**) corresponding to her **windward** side.

Close-hauled — A yacht is **close-hauled** when sailing by the wind as close as she can lie with advantage in working to windward.

Clear Astern and **Clear Ahead; Overlap** — A yacht is **clear astern** of another when her hull and equipment in normal position are abaft an imaginary line projected abeam from the aftermost point of the other's hull and equipment in normal position. The other yacht is **clear ahead**. The yachts **overlap** if neither is **clear astern**; or if, although one is **clear astern**, an intervening yacht **overlaps** both of them. The terms **clear astern**, **clear ahead** and **overlap** apply to yachts on opposite **tacks** only when they are subject to rule 42, Rounding or Passing Marks and Obstructions.

Leeward and **Windward** — The **leeward** side of a yacht is that on which she is, or, if **luffing** head to wind, was, carrying her mainsail. The opposite side is the **windward** side.

When neither of two yachts on the same **tack** is **clear astern**, the one on the **leeward** side of the other is the **leeward yacht**. The other is the **windward yacht**.

Proper course — A **proper course** is any course which a yacht might sail after the starting signal, in the absence of the other yacht or yachts affected, to **finish** as quickly as possible. The course sailed before **luffing** or **bearing away** is presumably, but not necessarily, that yacht's **proper course**. There is no **proper course** before the starting signal.

Mark — A **mark** is any object specified in the sailing instructions which a yacht must round or pass on a required side.

Obstruction — An **obstruction** is any object, including craft under way, large enough to require a yacht, if not less than one overall length away from it, to make a substantial alteration of course to pass on one side or the other, or any object which can be passed on one side only, including a buoy when the yacht in question cannot safely pass between it and the shoal or object which it marks.

PART IV

SAILING RULES WHEN YACHTS MEET

Helmsman's Rights and Obligations Concerning Right of Way

SECTION A—RULES WHICH ALWAYS APPLY

31 — Disqualification

1. A yacht may be disqualified for infringing a rule of Part IV only when the infringement occurs while she is **racing**, whether or not a collision results.

2. A yacht may be disqualified before or after she is **racing** for seriously hindering a yacht which is **racing**, or for infringing the sailing instructions.

32 — Avoiding Collisions

A right-of-way yacht which makes no attempt to avoid a collison resulting in serious damage may be disqualified as well as the other yacht.

33 — Retiring from Race

A yacht which realizes she has infringed a racing rule or a sailing instruction should retire promptly; but, when she persists in **racing**, other yachts shall continue to accord her such rights as she may have under the rules of Part IV.

34 — Limitations on the Right-of-Way Yacht to Alter Course

When one yacht is required to keep clear of another, the right-of-way yacht shall not (except to the extent permitted by rule 38.1, Right-of-way Yacht Luffing after Starting), so alter course as to prevent the other yacht from keeping clear; or to obstruct her while so doing.

35 — Hailing

A right-of-way yacht, except when **luffing** under rule 38.1, Luffing after Starting, should hail before or when making an alteration of course which may not be foreseen by the other yacht or when claiming the establishment or termination of an **overlap** at a **mark** or **obstruction**.

SECTION B — OPPOSITE TACK RULE

36 — Fundamental Rule

A **port-tack** yacht shall keep clear of a **starboard-tack** yacht.

SECTION C — SAME TACK RULES

37 — Fundamental Rules

1. A **windward yacht** shall keep clear of a **leeward yacht**.
2. A yacht **clear astern** shall keep clear of a yacht **clear ahead**.
3. A yacht which establishes an **overlap** to leeward from **clear astern** shall allow the **windward yacht** ample room and opportunity to keep clear, and during the existence of that **overlap** the **leeward yacht** shall not sail above her **proper course**.

38 — Right-of-Way Yacht Luffing after Starting

1. **Luffing Rights and Limitations.** After she has **started** and cleared the starting line, a yacht **clear ahead** or a **leeward yacht** may **luff** as she pleases, except that: —

     A **leeward yacht** shall not sail above her **proper course** while an **overlap** exists if, at any time during its existence, the helmsman of the **windward yacht** (when sighting abeam from his normal station and sailing no higher than the **leeward yacht**) has been abreast or forward of the mainmast of the **leeward yacht**.

2. **Overlap Limitations.** For the purpose of this rule: An **overlap** does not exist unless the yachts are clearly within two overall lengths of the longer yacht; and an **overlap** which exists between two yachts when the leading yacht **starts**, or when one or both of them completes a **tack** or **jibe**, shall be regarded as a new **overlap** beginning at that time.

3. **Hailing to Stop or Prevent a Luff.** When there is doubt, the **leeward yacht** may assume that she has the right to **luff** unless the helmsman of the **windward yacht** has hailed "Mast Abeam", or words to that effect. The **leeward yacht** shall be governed by such hail, and, if she deems it improper, her only remedy is to protest.

4. **Curtailing a Luff.** The **windward yacht** shall not cause a luff to be curtailed because of her proximity to the **leeward yacht** unless an **obstruction**, a third yacht or other object restricts her ability to respond.

5. **Luffing Two or More Yachts.** A yacht shall not **luff** unless she has the right to **luff** all yachts which would be affected by her **luff**, in which case they shall all respond even if an intervening yacht or yachts would not otherwise have the right to **luff**.

39 — Sailing Below a Proper Course

A yacht which is on a free leg of the course shall not sail below her **proper course** when she is clearly within three of her overall lengths of either a **leeward yacht** or a yacht **clear astern** which is steering a course to pass to **leeward**.

40 — Right-of-Way Luffing before Starting

Before a yacht has **started** and cleared the starting line, any **luff** on her part which causes another yacht to have to alter course to avoid a collision shall be carried out slowly and in such a way so as to give the **windward yacht** room and opportunity to keep clear, but before her starting signal, the **leeward yacht** shall not so **luff** above a **close-hauled** course, unless the helmsman of the **windward yacht** (sighting abeam from his normal station) is abaft the mainmast of the **leeward yacht**. Rules 38.3, Hailing to Stop or Prevent a Luff; 38.4, Curtailing a Luff; and 38.5, Luffing Two or more Yachts, also apply.

SECTION D — CHANGING TACK RULES

41 — Tacking or Jibing
[Tacking Too Close Rule]

1. A yacht which is either **tacking** or **jibing** shall keep clear of a yacht **on a tack**.

2. A yacht shall neither **tack** nor **jibe** into a position which will give her right of way unless she does so far enough from a yacht **on a tack** to enable this yacht to keep clear without having to begin to alter her course until after the **tack** or **jibe** has been completed.

3. A yacht which **tacks** or **jibes** has the onus of satisfying the race committee that she completed her **tack** or **jibe** in accordance with rule 41.2.

4. When two yachts are both **tacking** or both **jibing** at the same time, the one on the other's **port** side shall keep clear.

SECTION E — RULES OF EXCEPTION AND SPECIAL APPLICATION

When a rule of this section applies, to the extent to which it explicitly provides rights and obligations, it over-rides any conflicting rule of Part IV which precedes it except the rules of Section A — Rules Which Always Apply.

42 — Rounding or Passing Marks and Obstructions
[Buoy Room Rule]

When yachts either on the same **tack** or, after **starting** and clearing the starting line, on opposite **tacks**, are about to round or pass a **mark** on the same required side or an **obstruction** on the same side: —

When Overlapped

1.(*a*)   An outside yacht shall give each yacht **overlapping** her on the inside, room to round or pass it, except as provided in rules 42.1 (c), (d) and (e). Room includes room to **tack** or **jibe** when either is an integral part of the rounding or passing manoeuvre.

(*b*)   When an inside yacht of two or more **overlapped** yachts on opposite **tacks** will have to **jibe** in rounding a **mark** in order most directly to assume a **proper course** to the next **mark**, she shall **jibe** at the first reasonable opportunity.

(*c*)   When two yachts on opposite **tacks** are on a beat or when one of them will have to **tack** either to round the **mark** or to avoid the **obstruction**, as between each other rule 42.1 (a) shall not apply and they are subject to rules 36, Opposite Tack Fundamental Rule, and 41, Tacking or Jibing.

(*d*)   An outside **leeward yacht** with luffing rights may take an inside yacht to windward of a **mark** provided that she hails to that effect and begins to **luff** before she is within two of her overall lengths of the **mark** and provided that she also passes to windward of it.

(*e*)   [Anti-Barging Rule] When approaching the starting line to **start,** a **leeward yacht** shall be under no obligation to give any **windward yacht** room to pass to leeward of a starting **mark** surrounded by navigable water; but, after the starting signal, a **leeward yacht** shall not deprive a **windward yacht** of room at such a **mark** by sailing either above the first **mark** or above **close-hauled**.

When Clear Astern and Clear Ahead

2.(*a*)   A yacht **clear astern** shall keep clear in anticipation of and during the rounding or passing manoeuvre when the yacht **clear ahead** remains on the same **tack** or **jibes**.

(*b*)   A yacht **clear ahead** which **tacks** to round a **mark** is subject to rule 41, Tacking or Jibing, but a yacht **clear astern** shall not **luff** above **close-hauled** so as to prevent the yacht **clear ahead** from **tacking**.

Restrictions on Establishing and Maintaining an Overlap

3.(*a*)   A yacht **clear astern** shall not establish an inside **overlap** and be entitled to room under rule 42.1(a) when the yacht **clear ahead**: —

   (i)   is within two of her overall lengths of the **mark** or **obstruction**, except as provided in rules 42.3(b) and 42.3(c); or

   (ii)   is unable to give the required room.

(*b*)   The two lengths determinative of rule 42.3(a)(i) shall not apply to yachts, of which one has **tacked** in the vicinity of a **mark**, unless when the **tack** is completed the yachts are clearly more than two overall lengths from the **mark**.

(*c*)   A yacht **clear astern** may establish an **overlap** between the yacht **clear ahead** and a continuing **obstruction** such as a shoal or the shore, only when there is room for her to do so in safety.

(*d*) (i) A yacht **clear ahead** shall be under no obligation to give room
to a yacht **clear astern** before an **overlap** is established.

  (ii) A yacht which claims an inside **overlap** has the onus of satisfying the race committee that the **overlap** was established
in proper time.

(*e*) (i) When an outside yacht is **overlapped** at the time she comes
within two of her overall lengths of a **mark**, she shall continue to be bound by rule 42.1(a) to give room as required
even though the **overlap** may thereafter be broken.

  (ii) An outside yacht which claims to have broken an **overlap** has
the onus of satisfying the race committee that she became
clear ahead when she was more than two of her overall
lengths from the **mark**.

43 – Close-Hauled, Hailing for Room to Tack at Obstructions

1. **Hailing.** When two **close-hauled** yachts are on the same **tack** and
safe pilotage requires the yacht **clear ahead** or the **leeward yacht** to make
a substantial alteration of course to clear an **obstruction**, and if she intends
to **tack**, but cannot **tack** without colliding with the other yacht, she shall
hail the other yacht for room to **tack**, but she shall not hail and **tack**
simultaneously.

2. **Responding.** The hailed yacht at the earliest possible moment after
the hail shall either: —

(*a*) **tack**, in which case, the hailing yacht shall begin to **tack** either: —

  (i) before the hailed yacht has completed her **tack**, or

  (ii) if she cannot then **tack** without colliding with the hailed
yacht, immediately she is able to **tack**, or

(*b*) reply "You **tack**", or words to that effect, if in her opinion she
can keep clear without **tacking** or after postponing her **tack**.
In this case: —

  (i) the hailing yacht shall immediately **tack** and

  (ii) the hailed yacht shall keep clear.

  (iii) The onus shall lie on the hailed yacht which replied "You
tack" to satisfy the race committee that she kept clear.

3. **Limitation on Right to Room**

(*a*) When the **obstruction** is a **mark** which the hailed yacht can fetch,
the hailing yacht shall not be entitled to room to **tack** and the
hailed yacht shall immediately so inform the hailing yacht.

(*b*) If, thereafter, the hailing yacht again hails for room to **tack**, she
shall, after receiving it, retire immediately.

(*c*) If, after having refused to respond to a hail under rule 43.3(a), the
hailed yacht fails to fetch, she shall retire immediately.

44 – Yachts Returning to Start

1.(*a*) A premature starter when returning to **start**, or a yacht working
into position from the wrong side of the starting line or its
extensions, when the starting signal is made, shall keep clear
of all yachts which are **starting**, or have **started**, correctly,
until she is wholly on the right side of the starting line or its
extensions.

(*b*) Thereafter, she shall be accorded the rights under the rules of Part IV of a yacht which is **starting** correctly; but if she thereby acquires right of way over another yacht which is **starting** correctly, she shall allow that yacht ample room and opportunity to keep clear.

2. A premature starter while continuing to sail the course and until it is obvious that she is returning to **start**, shall be accorded the rights under the rules of Part IV of a yacht which has **started**.

45 — Yachts Re-rounding after Touching a Mark

1. A yacht which has touched a **mark** and is about to correct her error in accordance with rule 52.1, Touching a Mark, shall keep clear of all other yachts which are about to round or pass it or have rounded or passed it correctly, until she has rounded it completely and has cleared it and is on a **proper course** to the next **mark**.

2. A yacht which has touched a **mark**, while continuing to sail the course and until it is obvious that she is returning to round it completely in accordance with rule 52.1, Touching a Mark, shall be accorded rights under the rules of Part IV.

SECTION F—WHEN NOT UNDER WAY

46 — Anchored, Aground or Capsized

1. A yacht under way shall keep clear of another yacht **racing** which is anchored, aground or capsized. Of two anchored yachts, the one which anchored later shall keep clear, except that a yacht which is dragging shall keep clear of one which is not.

2. A yacht anchored or aground shall indicate the fact to any yacht which may be in danger of fouling her. Unless the size of the yachts or the weather conditions make some other signal necessary a hail is sufficient indication.

3. A yacht shall not be penalized for fouling a yacht in distress which she is attempting to assist or a yacht which goes aground or capsizes immediately ahead of her.

PART V

OTHER SAILING RULES

Obligations of Helmsman and Crew in Handling a Yacht

Except for rule 49, a yacht is subject to the rules of Part V only while she is **racing**.

49 — Fair Sailing

A yacht shall attempt to win a race only by fair sailing, superior speed and skill, and, except in team races, by individual effort. However, a yacht may be disqualified under this rule only in the case of a clear-cut violation of the above principles and only if no other rule applies.

50 — Ranking as a Starter

A yacht which sails about in the vicinity of the starting line between her preparatory and starting signals shall rank as a starter, even if she does not **start**.

51 – Sailing the Course

1.(*a*)   A yacht shall **start** and **finish** only as prescribed in the starting and finishing definitions, even if the committee boat is anchored on the side of the starting or finishing **mark** opposite to that prescribed in the sailing instructions.

(*b*)   Unless otherwise prescribed in the sailing instructions, a yacht which either crosses prematurely, or is on the wrong side of the starting line, or its extensions, at the starting signal, shall return and **start** in accordance with the definition.

(*c*)   Unless otherwise prescribed in the sailing instructions, when after a general recall, any part of a yacht's hull, crew or equipment is over the starting line during the minute before her starting signal, she shall thereafter pass on the course side of and around one of the starting **marks** and cross the starting line in the direction of the first **mark**.

(*d*)   Failure of a yacht to see or hear her recall notification shall not relieve her of her obligation to **start** correctly.

2.   A yacht shall sail the course so as to round or pass each **mark** on the required side in correct sequence, and so that a string representing her wake from the time she **starts** until she **finishes** would, when drawn taut, lie on the required side of each **mark**.

3.   A **mark** has a required side for a yacht as long as she is on a leg which it begins, bounds or ends. A starting **mark** begins to have a required side for a yacht when she **starts**. A finishing **mark** ceases to have a required side for a yacht as soon as she **finishes**.

4.   A yacht which rounds or passes a **mark** on the wrong side may correct her error by making her course conform to the requirements of rule 51.2.

5.   It is not necessary for a yacht to cross the finishing line completely. After **finishing** she may clear it in either direction.

6.   In the absence of the Race Committee, a yacht shall take her own time when she finishes, and report the time taken to the Race Committee as soon as possible. If there is no longer an established finishing line, the finishing line shall be a line extending from the required side of the finishing **mark** at right angles to the last leg of the course, and 100 yards long or as much longer as may be necessary to insure adequate depth of water in crossing it.

52 – Touching a Mark

1.   A yacht which either: –

(*a*)   touches: –

(i)   a starting **mark** before **starting**;

(ii)   a **mark** which begins, bounds or ends the leg of the course on which she is sailing; or

(iii)   a finishing **mark** after **finishing**, or

(*b*)   causes a **mark** vessel to shift to avoid being touched,

shall retire immediately, unless she claims that she was wrongfully compelled to touch it by another yacht, in which case she shall protest. However, unless otherwise prescribed in the sailing instructions, when the **mark** is surrounded by navigable water, a yacht may correct her error by making one complete rounding of the **mark**, leaving it on the required side without touching it, in addition to rounding or passing it as required to sail the course. In the case of a **mark** at the starboard end of the starting or finishing line, such complete rounding shall be clockwise, and at the port end of a starting or finishing line anti-clockwise.

2.   For the purposes of rule 52.1: Every ordinary part of a **mark** ranks as part of it, including a flag, flagpole, boom or hoisted boat, but excluding ground tackle and any object either accidentally or temporarily attached to it.